Our Only Hope

Eddie's Holocaust Story and the Weisz Family Correspondence

Studies in the Shoah
Volume XXX

Keith H. Pickus

UNIVERSITY PRESS OF AMERICA, ® INC.
Lanham • Boulder • New York • Toronto • Plymouth, UK

Copyright © 2008 by
University Press of America,® Inc.
4501 Forbes Boulevard
Suite 200
Lanham, Maryland 20706
UPA Acquisitions Department (301) 459-3366

Estover Road
Plymouth PL6 7PY
United Kingdom

British Library Cataloging in Publication Information Available

Library of Congress Control Number: 2007936547
ISBN-13: 978-0-7618-3920-0 (paperback : paper)
ISBN-10: 0-7618-3920-8 (paperback : paper)

For Eddie, in memory of his family,
Heinrich, Johanna and Ernst Weisz

Contents

Acknowledgements

Writing *Our Only Hope* was a labor of love with contributions from many people. I am indebted to John Thiessen of Bethel College in Newton, Kansas, who transcribed the hand- written letters into an electronic format. My colleague and dear friend, Anthony Gythiel, provided an initial translation of the letters from which I was able to work expeditiously. Margaret Dawe and Craig Miner of Wichita State University offered feedback during the early stages of writing that helped develop the book's narrative voice. Stephen McCann proofread the entire manuscript, and Kristie Bixby copy-edited it. My daughter, Lila Pickus, and a former student assistant, Mariam Mrevlishvili, transcribed the oral interviews with Eddie. Critical financial support for research and production was supplied by the Fairmount College of Liberal Arts and Sciences and the Office of Academic Affairs and Research at Wichita State University. Bill Bischoff, my boss these past six years, deserves special recognition for allowing me the time to continue my scholarship and for making the funds available that helped bring this book to fruition. As with everything that I do in life, writing *Our Only Hope* was nurtured by my wife, Deirdre O'Farrell. Her companionship and love are my most cherished gifts.

Most significantly, this book could not have been written without the involvement of Eddie Weiss, my uncle. When I began graduate studies in German and Jewish history at the University of Washington, Eddie began to speak openly with me about his family and their experience at the hands of the Nazis. Once, when visiting his home, he showed me the letters written to him by his father, mother, and brother, and he shared stories of their lives while looking through a photograph album. Years later, after accepting a position in the history department at Wichita State University, I approached Eddie about using the letters for a future project. Not only did he allow me to utilize the letters and his family photos in the book, he agreed to let me do an oral history of his life. Between 2000 and 2006, I conducted multiple interviews with Eddie, the content of which provided the additional details necessary to write this book. The time spent with Eddie these past seven years, both in his Van Nuys home and at Solley's delicatessen where we ate lunch each time I visited, has been precious. I cannot thank him enough for sharing his life's story with me. It is but a small token of my appreciation that I dedicate this book to my Uncle Eddie and to the memory of Heinrich, Johanna, and Ernst Weisz.

Introduction

In June, 1938, two months before his twenty-first birthday and five months before the pogrom known as the Night of Broken Glass shattered all remaining illusions of security for Jews remaining in Germany, Adolph "Eddie" Weisz embarked on a life-altering journey. He tearfully separated from his parents and younger brother at the *Anhalter Bahnhof* in Berlin, traveled by rail to Hamburg, and continued by boat to South Hampton, England, where, after seven days, he set sail for the United States. Pulling out of the Berlin station, Eddie began a "crying spell without end," one that continued almost until the train arrived in Hamburg. Recalling this event 67 years later, the days' emotions are still close to the surface.[1] As the oldest child of Heinrich and Johanna Weisz, Eddie was charged with clearing the way for his parents and younger brother, Ernst, to join him in the United States. From the moment that he fled Germany to escape the tightening noose of Nazi persecution, he worked tirelessly to facilitate his family's emigration. To his great disappointment, one that has haunted him throughout his life, Eddie's premonition about never seeing his family again proved correct. Heinrich, Johanna, and Ernst Weisz were killed by the Nazis and their accomplices. They were three of the six million Jews murdered during the Holocaust.

The tragic story of Jews in situations similar to that of Eddie and his family has often been told.[2] From the time that Hitler came to power in 1933, thousands of German Jewish parents sent their children to the United States and a myriad of other locations hoping to secure their future and facilitate their own emigration. Of the 300,000 Jews who fled Germany between 1933 and the outbreak of war in September, 1939, the great majority of them were in their twenties and thirties. Roughly fifty percent of those who remained were over fifty years old. The flight of younger German Jews was part of a conscious strategy to preserve the future of German Jewry. It was also a prag-matic response to an increasingly desperate situation. Emigration required people to uproot themselves from all that was familiar and dear to them, and to reestablish their lives in a new and foreign environment. Leaving the se-curity of one's home, family, and possessions for the unknown of a distant land where all familiar cultural signposts were different necessitated tremen-dous powers of adaptation. For German Jews in their forties, fifties, and six-ties who were raised and educated in Germany, who most likely had genera-tions of family members buried in local cemeteries and homes adorned with cherished heirlooms, fleeing their homeland was an option of last resort. Tragically, most of this cohort decided too late to seek refuge, when govern-ments and their bureaucrats slammed shut their points of entry for immi-grants. This was exactly the situation confronted by Heinrich and Johanna Weisz as they tried desperately to secure permission to join their son, Eddie, in the United States.

Younger Jews, who were less rooted in Germany and were more adaptable, had the wherewithal to re-imagine themselves in a foreign land far removed from the tyranny of the Nazi regime. They were often seen by foreign gov-ernments as having greater potential to contribute to their adopted homeland and less likely to need extensive financial assistance upon arrival. Eddie's own experience once he arrived in America in 1938 illuminates this phenom-enon. When Eddie's boat docked in New York and he disembarked, he was warmly embraced by his maternal uncle Armin Lobl, who had signed the nec-essary affidavits for him to emigrate to the U.S., and two of his father's sis-ters, Sophie and Rosa, all of whom lived in the area. After spending the evening in his aunts' second story Bronx apartment located above the candy store that they ran, Eddie looked for work on his second day in the United States. Within a matter of weeks he held multiple jobs and began sending money to his family. For the next three and half years, Eddie Weisz provided his parents and brother with the funds that enabled them to subsist as Jews in Nazi-dominated Europe. This simple act provided him partial solace as he tried desperately to facilitate his family's rescue.

The story that follows illuminates the lives of the Weisz family during the years 1938 to 1942. The narrative is pieced together from letters written to Eddie by Heinrich, Johanna, and Ernst Weisz before they were deported to Eastern Europe, and from interviews that I conducted with Eddie in his Los Angeles home. The purpose of the book is twofold. On one hand, it seeks to personalize the experience of Hitler's victims, to put a face on the lives of three of the six million Jews killed during the Holocaust. Much of our knowl-edge about the Holocaust is told from the perspective of the perpetrators, sur-vivors, and bystanders. Less is known about the daily lives of Jews who were the targets of the Nazi onslaught that deprived them of their citizenship, their livelihood, and, ultimately, their lives. The letters written by Eddie's family provide compelling details of daily life under Nazi oppression and the grow-ing anxiety associated with being separated from their oldest child. The book's second objective is to give voice to Eddie's story, the heart-wrenching tale of a young man's unsuccessful efforts to rescue his family. While the ba-sic outline of this experience has become increasingly well documented in re-cent years, each story is unique and deserves to be told. Teaching Holocaust history to university students on a regular basis for the past fifteen years has attuned me to the need to help students appreciate the impact of each life snuffed out by the Nazis. Every person killed during the Nazis' genocide of the Jews had parents, siblings, and friends. Their deaths created a void that re-mains to the present day, one that not only affects individuals like Eddie who lost his entire family but also those of us who live in the shadow of the Holo-caust. Giving voice to this story is a small step toward filling the void.

Heinrich, Johanna and Eddie Weisz
on a family vacation to Franzenbad, 1928.

The Weisz family on vacation in Marienbad, circa 1929.

Eddie, Johanna, Heinrich and Ernst Weisz, 1938.

NOTES

1. Oral Interview with Eddie Weisz, October 17, 2005.
2. David Clay Large's *And the World Closed its Doors*, (New York, 2003) details the heart wrenching experience of Max Schohl's futile efforts to secure the necessary paperwork to emigrate from Germany, and David Wyman's book. *The Abandonment of the Jews. America and the Holocaust 1941-1945*, (New York, 1984), illuminates the bureaucratic hurdles put up by members of the United State's State Department that made it extremely difficult for Jews to find refuge in the United States.

Chapter One

Leaving Home

Eddie Weisz was born on September 26, 1917, in Breslau, Germany, 14 months before the end of World War I. He was the oldest child of Heinrich and Johanna Weisz, both of whom were native to Hungary. Two years after Eddie's birth, the Weisz family moved to the Berlin suburb of Friedrickstein, a predominantly Gentile neighborhood with only a few Jewish families. On May 26, 1926, Eddie's younger brother and only sibling, Ernst, was born. The Weisz family lived a comfortable middle-class existence as citizens of Germany's Weimar Republic, the government formed following the collapse of the Hohenzollern monarchy in 1918. Heinrich Weisz was a wine and liquor merchant who catered to private individuals and restaurants, an occupation that required frequent trips away from Berlin. The income derived from this business afforded domestics to help with the cooking and cleaning, although the family always lived in rented apartments. Like many German Jews of the era, the Weisz family neither attended synagogue on a regular basis nor kept a kosher home. Yet, they abstained from eating pork, and they lit the Sabbath candles on Friday evenings and the Havdalah candles at sundown on Saturday. Memories of chicken soup, home-baked challah, and the smells of the Havdalah spice box are still etched in Eddie's mind sixty-seven years since he last shared these weekly rituals with his family.

When the Weisz family attended religious services on the High Holy days and the occasional Sabbath, they went to a synagogue located on Rykestrasse near their home in Berlin. The synagogue followed the customs of liberal Judaism common to German Jews at that time: men and women were seated separately, the worship service employed a choir but no organ music, and the Rabbi delivered a weekly sermon in German. To prepare for his Bar Mitzvah, Eddie studied twice weekly with the Rabbi to learn his Torah portion and Haftarah,

Bar Mitzvah Family Photo: Eddie is in the bottom row, third from the left.

Junior High School, Eddie is standing in the second row, fourth from the right.

the weekly prophetic reading chanted by the Bar Mitzvah. Eddie celebrated his Bar Mitzvah in September, 1930, a time marked by economic and political turmoil. The austere fiscal policies of Chancellor Heinrich Brüning did nothing to improve the economy, and they contributed to a dramatic rise in the number of Germans who were unemployed. The situation became so severe that Brüning became known as the 'Hunger Chancellor.' In spite of the economic troubles that plagued the country, the Weisz family joyously celebrated Eddie's Bar Mitzvah with family and friends from Berlin. His maternal uncle Armin, his mother's brother who lived in New York and would later sponsor Eddie's emigration to the United States, also attended the celebration.

Eddie's schooling was typical for Jews living in Berlin in the 1920s and 1930s: he began at the local *Grundschule* (public elementary school) at age six and transitioned to a *Realschule* (a public high school) when he was eleven years old. Eddie last attended school in 1933, the year that Adolph Hitler became Chancellor and the Nazis seized power. As one of only a few Jewish children at the Realschule, Eddie says that many employees of the school were not even aware that he was Jewish, a fact illuminated by the following incident. One day when discussing the physical attributes of "Aryans," the teacher called Eddie to the front of the class, put a ruler to his nose, and said, "You see, that's an Aryan nose!" A fellow student who knew that Eddie was not an Aryan shouted, "But he is a Jew Bastard!" Upon hearing this shocking revelation, the teacher "almost dropped the measuring tool she had in her hand." A short time later, Eddie left school and went to work as an apprentice in a leather goods store.

Life for Eddie and his family changed immediately after the Nazis seized power in January, 1933. Gentile children who had been friends with Eddie throughout his childhood began to avoid him, a development that propelled Eddie into a closer contact with Jewish athletic organizations. He has particularly fond memories of his membership in the Bar Kochba sports association, an organization that helped Eddie hone his boxing skills. On more than one occasion when local Hitler Youth taunted Eddie he utilized his boxing prowess to challenge his tormentors. In addition to altering the social relationships between Eddie and his Gentile friends, the Nazi seizure of power also affected his father's business. Hitler's brown-shirted storm troopers, the S.A., marked his wine shop as a Jewish store during the 1933 boycott, and five years later, the Nazi regime revoked his business license. As the Nazis' campaign against Jewish-owned businesses intensified, the Weisz family became more dependent upon Eddie's financial support. The loss of the family's primary income, coupled with the increasingly threatening daily existence confronted by German Jews, prompted the Weisz family to begin discussing the possibility of fleeing the country. They remained convinced, however, that they would be better off remaining in Germany until sometime in 1937 when Eddie was arrested by the German police for "illegally attempting to view a hockey game," and he was incarcerated for four days without his family knowing where he was. While in prison, Eddie's boxing skills were of no use to him. He was beaten repeatedly by police officers and had a number of his teeth knocked out. When he returned home, Heinrich and Johanna Weisz concluded that their family's safety was in jeopardy, and they decided to leave Germany.

Their decision to emigrate came at a time when doing so had become extremely difficult. The Nuremberg Laws of 1935 that deprived German Jews of their citizenship signaled to many Jews that they would be better off living elsewhere. Yet, in spite of a desire to rid Germany of its Jewish populace, Nazi officials placed significant obstacles in the path of those who had decided to flee. The most onerous of these were the restrictions placed on the wealth that Jews could take with them when they left the country. Between

Germany, 1936.

the Nazis' first efforts to restrict the outflow of wealth until the time that Eddie had obtained the necessary paperwork to leave the country, they reduced the amount of money that emigrating Jews could take with them to the absurd amount of ten marks per person. Those who sought refuge in the United States found their plans exacerbated by the bureaucratic hurdles set in place by U.S. immigration policy and State Department officials whose actions prevented thousands of Jews from obtaining the necessary visas. Regulations issued by the Hoover administration in 1930 required that all prospective immigrants have sufficient financial resources or backing to ensure that they would not become a "public charge." Since the Nazi regime prevented Jews from taking their wealth with them, those who wanted to immigrate to the United States needed to secure financial support from individuals living in the country. Affidavits of promised support or the prospect of future employment, even when guaranteed by an employer, were not sufficient by themselves to garner the coveted paperwork; the sponsors had to pledge assets to assure that the newly arriving immigrant would not become a public charge.

Recognizing that it would be impossible to secure the funding for all four family members to immigrate together, the Weisz family decided to send Eddie first. Although Eddie knew no English at the time, the family felt that he would have a much easier time making the transition to living in the United States than either of his parents. Eddie's mission was to establish himself as quickly as possible and to make the arrangements necessary for his family to follow. To secure the required affidavit of financial support the Weisz family turned to two German Jews who had immigrated earlier to America: a childhood friend of Eddie and Armin Lobl, Eddie's maternal uncle. After communicating with Eddie and his family in Berlin, the family friend traveled from Chicago, where he lived, to speak directly with Armin Lobl about the urgency of the situation for the Weisz family. While Armin Lobl did not have the resources to sponsor the entire family, he was willing to provide the necessary financial assistance for Eddie to obtain an entry visa into the United States. With the visa in hand, Eddie and his family turned to the task of securing the fare for the journey from England to the United States, a cost that they could not manage on their own. When questioned about this situation, Eddie recalls being sent to a wealthy Jewish family in Berlin, a couple from Turkey whom he had never met, to ask for their help. Not only did the strangers pay for his fare, they also sent Eddie home with additional money to aid the family. By spring, 1938, a time when the Nazi regime was making life increasingly difficult for the remaining Jews, all the pieces were in place for Eddie to leave Germany. Heinrich and Johanna Weisz prepared to send their oldest child to the United States hoping, desperately, to make the same journey themselves within the coming months.

Sometime in early June, 1938, Heinrich, Johanna, and Ernst Weisz accompanied Eddie to the Anhalter train station in Berlin. Eddie left home that morning with a small suitcase, a photograph album that contained family pictures, and ten marks. The only other details about the departure that are etched in his memory are the emotions of the day; the uneasiness associated with leaving home for the first time, a sense that he might never see his family again, and a pervasive loneliness that accompanied him as he traveled to Hamburg, where he boarded a boat for South Hampton, England. Upon arriving in England, Eddie made his way to London, where he contacted the Hebrew Immigrant Aid Society (HIAS), an organization that provided him food and lodging for the seven days that he remained in England before setting sail for the United States. On the journey to New York, Eddie shared a third class cabin with a man from India whom he had never met before. Although the ship was filled with tourists from England, Ireland, and Germany, Eddie spent most of the voyage by himself, reveling in the freedom associated with having escaped the threat of Nazism. He also remembers the near euphoria of having ample food to eat. The days of sharing a herring and a few potatoes for the family's main meal were behind him. Eddie would never again experience the hunger and deprivation that had become a daily occurrence for Jews living in Nazi Germany. The situation for Heinrich, Johanna, and Ernst Weisz was entirely different.

Eddie's departure initiated a new phase of life for the Weisz family, one marked by intense longing, expectation, and regular correspondence across the Atlantic ocean. From the day Eddie bid farewell to his family, the cards and letters that he sent on a regular basis became the life blood for his family in Germany, both for the hope of an eventual reunion that his communications kept alive and the money that Eddie often included with his messages. This situation is clearly evident from the first letters written by Johanna Weisz a few days after having bid farewell to her eldest son.

Berlin
13 June, 1938
(Johanna Weisz)

My beloved good child,

I write this letter to you with tears in my eyes, and I am continually very sad. When I left the train station I felt as if in a dream and my grief was limitless. We returned home on Friday, and when I saw your empty bed all the pain returned. As I stroke your pillow I always cry.

Dear Adi [a shortened form of Adolph used by Eddie's family in all its correspondence], my first thought each day when I awake and at night before I go to sleep is that I will see you again. I have read your dear letter and cards so often that I already know them by heart. Do not forget us my dear young man, and write me all that you do. I will always be with you in thought.

Hopefully you have endured the voyage well. I thank you very much for the promised money.

May God bless you my beloved child; make us and our relatives glad. I await with longing for more news from you. I greet and kiss you many, many times.

Your eternally loving Mutti.

Berlin

14 June, 1938
(Johanna Weisz)

My dear Adi,

Yesterday morning at 8:00 I received your money. You can only imagine that I cried again. It will be very hard for me to be without you. I have already used the money and I thank you very much, my good one, that you have made the effort.

Yesterday Papa went forth again and he returns Saturday when you disembark.

I have also obtained your card with the ship.

My thoughts are always with you. Write us often and my dear good boy, do not forget us. It is so lonely around me; I have interest in nothing. When I don't have to cook, then I will not do it.

Live well my dear child and remain healthy.

Many, many kisses from your loving Mutti.

As Johanna Weisz poured out her heart to her eldest son, Eddie lost no time acclimating himself to life in America and beginning the arduous process of securing affidavits for his family. When his boat docked in New York, Eddie gazed at the Statue of Liberty, not knowing anything about it at the time. He knew, however, that arriving in New York meant an end to the fear of living under the Nazi regime, a liberating feeling he describes as akin to having handcuffs removed. After making his way through Immigration, Eddie was warmly embraced by his maternal uncle, Armin Lobl, and two paternal aunts,

Sophie and Rosa. In his Aunts' candy store, Eddie encountered the American classics such as the *Baby Ruth*, *Snickers*, and the *Three Musketeers*. On his second day in New York, Eddie landed a job bussing dishes at a delicatessen across the street from Yankee Stadium, only to lose it three days later when he was caught eating an entire can of fruit cocktail, a delicacy that he had never experienced before. Almost immediately after this incident, Eddie began work cleaning carpets at the Coleridge Hotel, a job that placed him in frequent contact with other immigrants. The primary social outlet was a weekly dance held at the Empire Hotel on Columbus Circle. This venue also brought Eddie into contact with a man by the name of Eric Kowen who introduced him to the world of sales, a career that he remained in throughout his life. When questioned about the language skills necessary to communicate with an

New York, 1938.

English speaking clientele, Eddie says that the primary teaching aides were movies, signs, and the people whom he met. Within a few months after arriving in the United States, Eddie left his aunts' Bronx neighborhood for Manhattan, where he took a job as a shipping clerk for a jewelry store. This rapid acculturation and correspondingly busy life meant that Eddie was not able to send daily correspondence to his family, a situation that placed additional strain on his family in Berlin.

Berlin
30 June, 1938
(Johanna Weisz)

My beloved good Adi!

You can only imagine with what yearning and impatience I awaited news from you. I said to myself Wednesday or Thursday and, just yesterday, I received three letters from you and one from dear Uncle Armin. The arrival of your letters gave me a good deal to read, and I did not know where to start first.

My dear son you should know that I miss you much, even if I have to get used to this. God providing, we shall joyfully reunite soon.

I trust that you will not object that I have opened your locker and, moreover, I have sold the white trunk for seven marks. It made me very sad when they came to take the trunk away as it made me think so much about you my dear Adi.

Today I also received mail from dear Father. He writes [asking] whether I have already received mail from you. He returns home tomorrow, on Friday.

It pleases me greatly that you have been so lovingly accepted. I can imagine how you recognized Uncle Armin and greeted him. Tell me my dear, how is it with the money Uncle has deposited? Has Uncle Armin, even before you came, attended to the papers for Uncle Bernhard? I also will now begin with learning English.

Everything my dear Adi has now turned out well for you as you have undertaken it. I wish that God may bless everything you start; be happy my dear child, you deserve it. Perhaps as I write to you, you have a position already; that would be splendid. How I wish the day would be here when you write you already have papers for us. But perhaps I will have to wait so long.

On Tuesday, 28 June, shortly before midnight, Uncle Jojo left for Prague. He was at the consulate, and he told the gray haired [official] that he wanted to make an application. You know that it takes a long time until that is attained. Father and Uncle Bernhard have persuaded him not to wait for an application and to travel, instead, as he has done. I accompanied him to the station. During the last two weeks when he was with us he complained constantly that he had not heard from you in spite of his expectations. I will send him a letter as soon as I know his address. [Coincidentally] a letter from him also came today from Prague. He writes that he was with the community there, and they have given him four meal cards. Furthermore, they advised him to travel to Pressburg where German is also spoken, while in Prague there is only Czech. It grieves me now that he is so alone.

I will stop for today and let Ernst write. Greetings to all dear relatives. Dear good Adi, take care of yourself. Be well my dear Adi.

I kiss you many times.
Your loving Mutti.

Johanna Weisz's letter clearly communicates an intense yearning to be reunited with her son, and it is clear that, shortly after Eddie left home, she was already living for his letters. They had become the lifeline connecting her to her "dear Adi." Johanna Weisz's longing to be reunited with her eldest son is tempered by her pride for him, particularly the positive impression that he has made on family members living in the United States. She takes solace in imagining Eddie with her brother and two sisters-in-law. Family gatherings are the centerpiece of her life. Frau Weisz's concern for her family's well-being extends far beyond her husband and sons. She worries about her brother Jojo, who now lives alone in Prague, and other family members who, like herself, must also wait for Eddie to secure their affidavits. Much is riding on Eddie's ability to obtain the necessary emigration paperwork, and the extended Weisz family living in Europe is acutely aware of this as they adjust to the increasing pressure of living under Nazi domination. While Eddie may have escaped the direct threat of Nazi brutality, it continued to cast a dark shadow on the lives of his family.

Chapter Two

From Berlin to Prague

In the months preceding Eddie's departure, the Weisz family spoke often of their increasingly difficult living situation. From the time that Adolf Hitler and his Nazi Party took power in January 1933, the regime subjected German Jews to a legislative assault that rapidly undermined their legal and economic status. In April 1933, the Nazis passed the first of many laws designed to restrict German citizenship and exclude Jews and other foreign nationals from the civil service. They also instituted a national boycott against Jewish owned business. Although the boycott was ultimately abandoned, some of Heinrich Weisz's clients stopped doing business with him, and the family became increasingly dependent upon Eddie's wages to feed and clothe the family. The passage of the Nuremberg Citizenship Laws in 1935 completely deprived German-born Jews of their citizenship, and they provided the framework necessary for the Nazi regime to rid Germany of "foreign born Jews." Since both Heinrich and Johanna Weisz were born in "Czechoslovakian" towns,[1] this aspect of the Nuremberg Laws directly affected the Weisz family.

After a brief lull in the legislative campaign against the Jews that coincided with preparations for the 1936 Olympic Games, the Nazis intensified their assault on German Jewry in 1938. Jewish passports were branded with the letter "J," Jewish men were required to assume the middle-name of "Israel" and Jewish women the middle-name "Sarah." Once fully implemented, these and other legal restrictions deprived Heinrich Weisz of the identity papers necessary to travel for business, a blow that made it impossible for him to continue working. The prospect of being completely unemployed sealed Heinrich Weisz's decision to forsake Berlin for Prague, a place he thought would provide temporary refuge before immigrating to the United States. Little did he know that events would quickly outpace them, and before long, the Nazis' grip on his family would extend to their new home in Czechoslovakia. This is the backdrop against which the letters written between July and September 1938 were penned. The painful yearning to reunite with Eddie and news about life without him that punctuate the entire correspondence merge with the details and anxiety associated with the impending move to Prague.

Berlin
7 July, 1938
(Johanna Weisz)

My beloved good Adi,

I have been longing to hear news from you, and when I arrived home today, I received your dear letter in the second post. As you know, dear Father is presently away from home, but when I go to meet him on Friday, I will give him your letter to read first thing.

Hopefully you are getting along fine with the people with whom you live. My dear young one, countless times I think of you. I have one wish, to remain healthy and to see you. It is very nice of Uncle Armin to pay for your room. Bring him only joy my dear child so that I can be even more proud of you. You should also begin to save money. I know that you are not frivolous, but do not allow yourself to be seduced into that by Elias [Eddie's childhood friend who had emigrated earlier to the U.S.]. It is very calming for me to know that all is well with you.

Have you fulfilled all [your] tasks? Were you with Mr. Berhrend and what has he said? I was happy to read in your letter that you have already found a job. Also my Adi, it pleases me that the food tastes good to you. I thought we would be lucky and see you first, but instead it will be Uncle Bernhard. Why is that? Before you arrived, did Uncle Armin arrange for the papers?

This week I will go to the English teacher to speak with him. Can you understand [the English spoken]? My dear boy, apricots are in season again, but I have not yet made any dumplings. My eater of dumplings is too far from me. God knows when I will see you again. You are my entire thought. Soon you will have been away for four weeks. We are all healthy, although I have headaches more often. That is from thinking too much. When I have you around me, I will be back in order.

I have spoken today with Mrs. Frankel who complains that Elias does not send her money or write at all. The last time he wrote was June 8th; tell him he should not neglect his parents in this way. It is nice that you have written to Uncle Adolf. I also had mail from him. Do you spend much time with Elias?

Be very frugal my good boy. I will stop for today. In my thoughts I am always with you. I kiss you many, many times.

Your eternally loving Mutti.

Give our best regards to all relatives.

Berlin
12 July, 1938
(Johanna Weisz)

My dear good Adi,

I read your letter of June 26th with great interest. It is always a holiday for me when I have mail from you. Certainly, I am still in low spirits. You, my good boy, are our entire hope. I only have the ardent desire to see you soon. There is no reason for us to stay here my dear Adi. Father will only be allowed to remain in his business until 30 September 1938 when, then, there will be no more identity cards for travelers. We have given notice that we will leave our apartment at this time, and we will certainly sell the furniture. I do not feel sad about selling the furniture; rather, that we acquired it with such difficulty.

Yesterday we were with Fischbein, and I read him the letter about his relatives. The young man has obtained the affidavit that was signed by the niece of Mrs. Fischbein. Uncle Bernhard has received notice from the local help society that dear Aunt Sofie and dear Aunt Rosa are eligible for citizenship. As dear Father told me yesterday, he will also write to Aunt Sofie. As you see, our time here is very busy. The few weeks that remain for us in Germany will also soon be gone.

Kindermann was here also and has inquired about you. My good Adi, I also was with Mr. Moller, who wishes you the best. He also gave me 50 Reichsmarks, and you can imagine how very glad I was to receive it. However, I gave the money to Mrs. Fischbein, for, as you know, she lent me the money for you.

Give Uncle Armin my warmest greetings. Have you given him the pictures of the graves? Blessed Grandmother has been dead for one year already. There is nothing more for today my dear Adi.

Remain healthy and take good care. I kiss you innumerable times.

Your forever loving Mutti.

Write soon my good son.

Berlin
27 July, 1938
(Johanna Weisz)

My dear good Adi!

Your mail finally arrived, and the letters of the 8th and the 12th arrived at the same time. It pleases me greatly to read your dear letters. When I pick father up at the train station, he always reads them right away.

I miss you very much my dear boy. I have always told you that I was not certain how I would carry on without you, but for the time being, it goes well. The thought of a beautiful reunion with you helps as well.

Yes, your room is fairly empty, and we are beginning to sell the furniture. When I find a one-room apartment, we will have enough [furniture], especially since we will keep the bedroom furniture. We will give notice on the house for 1 September, as father can only work until 30 September. It has become very difficult for us, but dear father manages to provide all that we need. All of the other obligations, however, create a heavy burden.

When there is no more work for father, it is our intention to travel to Prague and stay there, my dear Adi, until we have the good luck to come to you. The only downside to Prague is that there is no help-association and the cost of traveling. Once in Prague, we will have to be very frugal with our money.

Dear father had already advised Uncle Jojo to move to Prague. Once there, he met the acquaintance of an Italian man who makes ice cream. This man taught the business to Uncle Jojo, and he has already begun to earn a nice income. We had a letter from him during the past week.

Berlin
6 August, 1938
(Heinrich Weisz)

My dear Adi!

Your dear letter pleased us greatly, and I fail to recognize all the good that you do for us. But unfortunately, unfortunately, things always turn out differently than one thinks. As I wrote to you in my last letter, I must give up my identity card on 30 September. Not only will I no longer be able to travel, but my ability to earn a livelihood will also be finished.

The American Consulate is now so overrun with applications that one can hardly get an appointment before January or February, 1939. Even if things go well, we will not be able to join you before March-April 1939. Our plan is to remain here until the beginning of October and then move, temporarily, to Prague. However, it probably will happen that the papers from Uncle Armin will be sent to the address of Uncle Adolf in Hlohowec. If this is not the case, we will have to wait until we have secured housing in Prague, and then you can secure the papers for us. This is the way it is my dear young man and not otherwise. Hopefully you understand.

On 1 September, we will give up our house and rent a small house until we leave. Unfortunately, we must sell everything cheaply because we can not get much for our beautiful things. All this really does not matter since the main things are that we remain healthy, bread is being baked everywhere, and people cook with water. The [other] important thing for us is that you are doing well. Mother and I are very pleased that you have obtained employment, and I am convinced that you are already finding your way [in America] in spite of the initial difficulties.

We continue to work diligently to learn English. Every Sunday, Mr. Gottmann comes to our home to help us make progress with our English. It will be a real pleasure to be with you speaking English.

Dear young one, be patient. Do not worry yourself sick, everything will be fine. I will write you more good things in my next letter, but I will await your answer.

For today, give my regards to all the relatives.

With an affectionate embrace and 10,000 heartfelt kisses.

Your sincerely loving Papa.

Berlin
14 August, 1938
(Heinrich Weisz)

My dear Adi!

Yesterday we received your letter of 2 August, and it pleases us to learn that you are healthy and well. My heartfelt thanks go to my sisters, your dear aunts, for all of their hard work and effort on your behalf.

As I have already written to you, I must give up my business. We will remain here until 16 September. In the event that the papers can be sent here [while we are still in Germany], you should send them to #4 Friedenstrasse, so that the papers can be here on time. In case matters slow down, send the papers to me in Prague, in care of the Jewish community. As soon as you receive this letter, let us know if the papers have been sent.

Even if we receive the papers before we travel to Prague, we would not be able to travel directly to the USA. The American consulate is so overwhelmed with inquiries that we probably would not be able to get away before March-April of 1939.

In the meantime we will diligently learn English and hope that you, my good boy, already are so far advanced that we will be able to manage easily.

As I have already written to you, we are only keeping our bedroom furniture. You can imagine that it is not easy to give away everything. We are healthy and that is the essential thing, praise God.

In closing, please give my best greetings to the aunts, uncles, and girls.

Your loving Papa.

Berlin
14 August, 1938
(Johanna Weisz)

My beloved good son,

I see that you are well provided with writing paper. Mrs. Frankel was with us yesterday. I have also read your letter, and I look forward to the promised pictures. It is also very nice that you have written to Uncle Jup.

We have sold some furniture for 30 Reichsmarks. If it is possible, I plan to bring my crystal and my good tableware with me. It would be too expensive to move all of the furniture, and we will only take the bedroom furniture with us to Prague.

Uncle Jacob will accompany us to Prague; what could he do here all by himself? We know that we will have to look for another English teacher since Gottmann has been assigned to the English consulate.

Today we are in Wendenschloss with Mr. Fischbein. Papa lies in the deckchair reading a newspaper. Little Ernst is in the neighborhood with some other youngsters. On Mondays and Wednesdays he goes to training at the Friedrichstrasse facility, which he enjoys very much. He also speaks about you often, my son.

Do you know what my dear Adi? I think that it is good that your late Grandmother is no longer living since all of us will depart.

Now I wait longingly for your next letter. Remain healthy and take care of yourself.

Greetings to all our dear ones. I kiss you often my beloved Adi.

Your intimately loving Mutti.

Berlin
25 August, 1938
(Johanna Weisz)

My dear good Adi,

I write this letter with great anxiety about you. I already have a headache from thinking too much, waiting in vain, from one mail to the next, for news from you. You had promised me to write weekly. You wrote the last card on 8 August and we received it on 18 August. Since then nothing. Yet you know how anxious I am. Father has also written. We will remain in this house until 15 September. In order for me to receive additional mail from you at this address, you must write your last letter on 2 September.

Here everything looks as though we are already moving. The floor is entirely empty, as is your room. Mrs. Hoch took your bed and the carpets. I was extremely sad when they carried out your bed, as my thoughts were with you over the great water. The beautiful wood plates are with Hoh. It is depressingly sad when one has to sell one possession after another, especially when we get so little money for it all. But what can we do? We cannot take these things with us. The coal merchant purchased the dining room lamp for 25 Reichsmarks.

We will move to Prague sometime around 20 September. Uncle Jojo rejoices already, as he looks forward to having a home again. He has already written to tell me that I must cook him [his favorite dish] when I am there. I have also given the winter coat that you sent to Uncle Adolf.

My dear son, where are the pictures you promised? I already wait for mail from you, and I long to see the photos. I hope that you are healthy and also have work.

In the short time that we are still here, I will go frequently to visit the [family] gravesite. Next time, I will take Ernst with me, and we will plant something green to grow on the tomb so that it will not be so empty [in our absence]. At present, I am pleased that you have made pictures.

Ernst boxes on Monday and Wednesdays, and he is joined by Erich.

How are the relatives doing, and how goes it with Elias? Give them all my warmest greetings.

(The following lines were written in English.)

How do you do?

When do you go home.

Johanna and Heinrich Weisz, 1938.

What do you say about my English? We are still learning it.

Be well my dear Adi, and stay in good health for me. I wish you all the conceivable good.

Take care of yourself. I kiss you countless times.

Your tenderly loving Mutti.

Berlin
29 August, 1938
(Johanna Weisz)

My good-hearted dear Adi!

I have read your letter with tears in my eyes. I received it on Friday with the first mail, and I brought it to Father [when I picked him up] at the train station. I was so pleased to read your letters again. What has happened to the photos that you promised? I long to at least see pictures of you.

Ernst is off at boxing training. He enjoys it every bit as much as you.

Now, my dear Atze, pay heed to what I have to tell you. You are to keep the papers with you until we write you with the Prague address. You will then send them directly to us in Prague. The American consulate is so overwhelmed with applications that they are accepting no more until March. We will leave for Prague on approximately 20 September, and we will move from this house on 15 September.

The dining room furniture is already sold. Mrs. Hoh took it for 225 Reichsmarks. I cried because it pained me to sell our beautiful things. Also, I could be happy if I were already with you. If only we will remain healthy and have a joyful reunion.

Now, my beloved child, moving from you to us. Do not be angry when I tell you not to send us money, but to save it for yourself. When we need some for travel, I will certainly write to you.

After receiving this letter, write to us immediately so that I have mail from you until 14 September. We have received mail from Uncle Jojo [in Prague]. He writes that he trades on the large market, which is open from 3:00 A.M. until 7:00 A.M., and that it resembles the New Market in Berlin. He says that things are going very well for him, and he is looking forward to our arrival. I can make him [his favorite food]. What, my dear son, shall I make for you first?

My dear Adi, in my sleepless nights I think of you as tears cover my face and the pillow. Your absence is heavier to bear than what one might imagine.

However, I know that it is good for you and that you will master life. May God bless you my beloved son.

How are things with the dear aunts? Hopefully they are both in good health. Give them my heartfelt greeting and do not forget dear Uncle Armin.

Be well for me my dear Adi.

I kiss you countless times.

Your faithful Mutti.

Take good care of yourself.

Berlin
15 September, 1938
(Johanna Weisz)

My dearly beloved good Adi!

I will not let today pass by without writing to you, my good young son. Your affidavit lies before me. I have looked at it very often, and I have read your dear name with full devotion.

Today we left our house and moved to a furnished room. I have been up since 5:00 A.M. because changing residences is very hard work.

We thank the aunts very much for their efforts. It pains me so to hear of dear Aunt Sofie. I know you are nice to her so that she will not be so sad.

My dear son, when you hold this letter in your good hands, we will probably be in Prague. I hope this is the case. It [life in Germany] is very dreadful. Tomorrow, (Friday) when dear father comes home, I will tell him now that we should leave quickly. I am so fearful and at the same time nostalgic for you, my dear Adi. When we leave from here, we will only be able to take our clothes with us, everything else must stay here.

Your birthday is on the first day of Rosh Hashanah, and it is the first time that you will be away on both your birthday and the Holy day. It will be a very difficult day for me. My beloved child, I wish you every imaginable good and beautiful thing. May God bless you and make you fortunate. Remain my good son and my pride.

What type of work do you have my dear Adi? Live well my good son and take good care of yourself. You must always think of me. I kiss you my dear Adi. I am your eternally loving mother. It is now eleven at night here. Good night my Adi. Many hearty greetings to all of the dear relatives.

(Written at the end of the letter by Eddie's brother, Ernst.)

Dear Adi,

I received your dear letter. On Thursday, I boxed with Erich in the August-strasse. I gave Erich a real upper cut that knocked him down and he was counted out. The whole family was there.

I also want to wish you a good and healthy life for your 21st birthday. I hope that we will all be together soon.

Ernst

While Eddie spent his first months in the United States reveling in the freedom of having escaped the Nazi threat, eating all that he desired and soaking up the sights, sounds, and smells of New York, his family struggled to keep their lives together. Eddie's departure clearly exacted a psychological toll on his mother whose longing for her eldest son is evident from the first letters that she penned. Thoughts of Eddie and an eventual reunion preoccupy Johanna Weisz's waking hours, and his absence is the source of great concern. Disabling headaches and deep melancholy make their first appearance shortly after Eddie's departure. Eddie's move to the United States also meant that the family had to make ends meet without his wages. The references to "saving money" and being "frugal" speak both of the need for Eddie to acquire the funds necessary to secure his parents' emigration and the increasingly strained financial situation faced by the family in Berlin. From the time that Eddie left school in 1933 until he emigrated to America, a good portion of his monthly income helped support the family. In fact, his contributions became increasingly critical as Heinrich Weisz's business gradually dwindled. The situation would reach a crisis at the end of September when Heinrich Weisz would no longer be able to work in Germany.

Many of the letters written by Heinrich and Johanna Weisz mention efforts to secure the paperwork necessary to emigrate to the United States, and they detail the growing frustration with the bureaucratic hurdles faced by all. By mid-summer, 1938, the Weisz family was acutely aware that they had no future in Germany. The move to Prague was an attempt to provide some breathing space between themselves and the Nazis until they could reunite with Eddie in America. Heinrich and Johanna Weisz's letters to their son in early August provide a glimpse into the challenges faced by German Jews hoping to emigrate to the United States and the stress associated with waiting to secure the requisite paperwork. Like the successful business man that he was, Heinrich Weisz tried to anticipate every contingency and prepare accordingly. Unfortunately, Jews living in Nazi Germany no longer controlled their destiny. Caught between the bureaucratic red tape created by the United States Department of State and the hurdles erected by the Nazi regime, the Weisz family and, thousands of German Jews in similar situations, were dependent on others for help. They had been rendered virtually powerless, and their options were limited. Caught in a whirlwind of events and directives beyond their control, Heinrich and Johanna Weisz took every conceivable step to maintain some semblance of normalcy. They encouraged their youngest son, Ernst, to participate in sports and other activities that took place at the local Jewish community center. They also visited regularly with friends and relatives and attempted to preserve some quality of life by selling their cherished possessions. As we now know, there was no shortage of potential customers for the Weisz's worldly goods. While Jewish businesses were "Aryanized" and German Jews prepared to leave Germany by selling what they could not take with them, thousands of German Gentiles benefited from this enterprise. The level of complicity in the Nazi plunder of Jewish wealth was extremely high.

Yet, in spite of these extremely difficult and anxious developments, Heinrich and Johanna Weisz remained optimistic. After all, they had their health, it was still possible to feed the family, and Eddie had established a beachhead on American soil for the Weisz family to follow. With perseverance and a bit of luck, the family would reunite in a couple of months. Eddie's successful transition to life in the United States bode well for the family's survival strategy. When Heinrich, Johanna, and Ernst Weisz left for Prague at the end of September, 1938, they had reason to hope for a future reunion with Eddie in the United States. As they made their way across the border from Germany to Czechoslovakia, they could not possibly have known that their reprieve from the Nazi regime would last less than seven months. This crushing blow is detailed in future correspondence.

NOTE

1. Both Heinrich and Joanna Weisz were born in Hungarian towns, Verbo and Dalgost. The geo-political changes of 1919 incorporated both villages into the newly established nation of Czechoslovakia, a situation that rendered both of them Czech nationals according to Nazi citizenship laws.

Chapter Three

The First Prague Fall, October–December 1938

In the summer months before the Weisz family moved to Prague, Adolf Hitler began to publicly agitate on behalf of ethnic Germans living in the western portion of Czechoslovakia known as the Sudetenland. Having already brought Austrian Germans into the 'Greater German Reich' with the Anschluss in March 1938, Hitler focused his attention on the Sudeten Germans. At the precise moment when Heinrich, Johanna, and Ernst Weisz were making final preparations for their move to Prague in September 1938, Hitler ratcheted up his rhetoric by demanding "self-determination" for the Sudetenland, an announcement that sparked public unrest in Czechoslovakia and the declaration of martial law. The deteriorating situation led to meetings between Hitler and British Prime Minister Neville Chamberlain, the second of which was held in Bad Godesberg, Germany. At this meeting, Hitler insisted that German troops be allowed to occupy the Sudetenland and that territory inhabited primarily by Poles and Magyars be returned to Poland and Hungary. Britain and France rejected both demands.

The growing conflict between Germany and its Czechoslovakian neighbor brought Europe to the precipice of war. Urged by President Franklin Delano Roosevelt and Benito Mussolini to peacefully settle their disputes, representatives from Britain, France, Italy, and Germany met on 29 September in Munich to discuss Czechoslovakia's future. Representatives from the Czechoslovakian democracy, however, were forced to wait in the corridor outside the meeting room while the European powers debated their fate. Anxious to avoid war at all costs, England and France passively acquiesced to Hitler's demands and signed the Munich Pact on 30 September, 1938. This agreement, which authorized German troops to occupy the Sudetenland, marked the epitome of Chamberlain's appeasement policy. When German troops marched into the

Sudetenland on 1 October, 1938, the distance between the Nazi regime and the Weisz family narrowed considerably. The much anticipated temporary safe haven of Prague suddenly became much more precarious. The enemy was literally at the gate.

The first letters written by Heinrich and Johanna Weisz from Prague provide a stark view of the pressures associated with relocating to Czechoslovakia and a fascinating commentary on the days' historical events. Heinrich Weisz's lamentations speak volumes. He was separated from his beloved eldest son, his living conditions were greatly diminished, and his inability to speak Czech made finding work extremely difficult. Without work and no cash savings to fall back on, Heinrich Weisz had no option but to sell his remaining possessions to provide food for his family. While food costs were cheaper in Prague than Berlin, a family still needed money to survive. The strange and sad feelings of relocation experienced by Eddie in New York were shared by his father in Prague.

Johanna Weisz's letters demonstrate how much of her time was preoccupied with waiting. She waited impatiently for letters from Eddie which, because of the move to Prague and the increasingly strained diplomatic atmosphere, took upwards of four weeks to be delivered. Life had also become exceedingly stressful. The departure from Berlin had created friction within the extended family when Johanna Weisz tried to arrange the final days' lodging with one of her brothers. Celebrating the Jewish New Year (Rosh Hashanah) and the Day of Atonement (Yom Kippur), the first without Eddie, is described in poignantly painful detail. Commenting that she was not "in the right" Temple and that Eddie's most recent letter was her "prayer book" indicates the pain of being separated from her eldest son.

Eddie's support role took on new significance once the family moved to Prague. The reverence for Eddie's letter bearing cash and the detailed attention given to describing how best to conduct similar future transactions suggest the beginning of a new phase in the lives of the Weisz family: Eddie's role as 'life-line' was no longer future-oriented. He would become their most important source of financial support.

In discussing this situation with Eddie, he offered a fascinating account of his efforts to provide money for his parents. At first he simply put cash in a letter without worrying about censors stealing it. Shortly after receiving the letter from his mother about the dangers of sending American currency through the post, Eddie met a Czechoslovakian man named Mr. Band who, like Eddie, had not been able to take cash with him when he immigrated to the United States. Apparently, Mr. Band had left a sizable bank account behind in his Czech homeland. Unable to secure steady employment in New York and needing to supplement his cash flow, Mr. Band devised a plan to improve the financial situation for himself and Eddie's parents. He proposed that Eddie pay him ten dollars a month in exchange for him releasing Czech funds to Eddie's parents in Prague. Beginning in late fall, 1938, Heinrich and Johanna Weisz were able to collect 500 Czech Kroner per month from Mr. Band's bank in Prague. This money, according to Eddie, provided his parents with some of life's basics: food, clothing, and shelter. When asked how it made him feel knowing that he was able to support his family, Eddie commented, "It made me feel good. I would say satisfaction; not really satisfaction, it made me feel good. Mentally it did something for me to do that. Yes, the feeling of helping my parents was better than nothing." The monthly payments from Mr. Band's bank account continued until March 1939, when the Nazis swallowed the Czech provinces of Bohemia and Moravia. Just before the Nazis entered Prague, Mr. Band released his bank account's remaining funds to Heinrich Weisz. Not only did this move prevent his money from being confiscated by the Nazis, it also provided a cash reserve that supported Eddie's family for a number of months. This money, however, was one of the few bright spots in an increasingly difficult existence.

Prague
3 October, 1938
(Heinrich Weisz)

My beloved son!

I received your letter dated the 11th that was addressed to Uncle Jojo. My dear child, you write that your mood is strange or, perhaps, best described as sad. Unfortunately, that is also the case with us, as everything that a man loves is torn apart. I will not complain my son, for one must accept one's fate as it presents itself.

We have been here for about 14 days, and we live in an apartment with furniture. You can imagine how [things have changed for us.] But the main thing is that we are all healthy, thanks be to God. We had only just arrived when there was a threat of war. We hardly had one day of light when we were confronted again with uncertainty. Now the whole affair is over.

This week I will see if I can get some work, which is very difficult for me since Czech is not a Slavic language. I will also go to see the American Consulate and see what the problem is. Mine and mother's most sincere wish is that, God willing, we will be together. I want nothing else from life.

It is very beautiful here in Prague, in spite of the limited conditions. Food items are half the price that they are in Berlin. Still, however, one must earn money. We will see. We have sold the wardrobe and the furs. Thanks be to God, we have enough to eat and all the necessary things.

As soon as I have news I will write you. The surrender of the German territories has created a very gloomy mood, which is completely understandable. It is a shame what they have done to this democracy.

Dear Adi, please write to us soon. You and all of the beloved relatives have done so much on our behalf.

Greetings and kisses.

Your loving Papa.

Prague
28 October, 1938
(Johanna Weisz)

My beloved good Adi!

You must already be waiting for news from us, but the mail takes so long now that one really loses patience. Your dear letter of 22 September took exactly four weeks to reach us.

We handed in the papers [to the American Consulate] on 18 September, and the lady who took them from us said it would be five to six months before everything is settled. We must have looked very disappointed, but perhaps we can leave earlier. God willing, everything will go well and we will have a joyful reunion.

My dear son, you asked [in an earlier letter] why we did not spend the last days in Berlin with Aunt Rosa. Uncle B. told dear Papa that doing so would create a lot of fuss. I have much to write about this, but I am hopeful that you will hear all of this in person from us. In any event, we went to 9 Hufelandstrasse where we paid 30 Reichsmarks for a few days lodging. We left Berlin on 20 September.

Ernst is doing well. He likes to eat and drink. I do not let him go outside after school. It is not worth the worry. He speaks of you a great deal, and he is growing up.

We received a few letters from Uncle Adolf. When we have the good fortune to travel to you, we will first have to say farewell to Uncle Adolf. Uncle Bernhard wrote us a card this week from Dresden. He could not get any further because the borders were closed. Hopefully, traffic will soon be restored and he will be able to come [from Berlin to Prague].

My beloved son, we are very proud of you. We read your recent letter with great joy and tears in our eyes. Weren't you with Uncle Armin in Temple? For us the High Holy Days were very empty and vacant. If only things were entirely different. We too were in Temple, but it was not the right one. Your dear letter was my prayer book. I thought of you continuously and prayed to God that we would all be together for the next High Holy Days. My good son, have you found the flat cakes that you enjoy so much? It pleases me that the dear aunts are so good to you. I wish them all the best and also that I could return the favor.

Now, my dear Adi, the money that you sent brought us great joy. Uncle Jupp came in the evening and placed both the money and the letter on the table. I cried a great deal, and dear father was also completely moved. He said, "The dear young man!" After that, dear father went out with us to eat sausage. Letters are being censored and, luckily, yours was not opened. In the event that it will be possible for you to send money again, send only a check in a registered letter. A [regular] letter can easily get lost when it comes in the wrong hand.

It is very unfortunate that we have to wait so long to leave from here. The load upon us here is tremendous. The lost German territories means that refugees arrive in groups, and as a result, the government has issued a one-year work prohibition for recently arrived [refugees]. We have jumped out of the frying pan into the fire. You can only imagine the worries father has. I often say that if Adi would see us this way, he would weep. Everything my dear boy is so completely different for us. Now I understand the letters of lamentation that Aunt Gotta sent us, although we are here in joy. I thank God that you know nothing of all this. Our expectations have become very modest, yet we hope that this time will pass. You are our entire hope my dear son. I will stop for now.

Write to us in detail [all that you do]. Remain healthy for me. I kiss you many times.

Your sincerely loving Mutti.

Prague
10 November, 1938
(Johanna Weisz)

My dear golden son,

I am here alone in the house, and as is often the case, my thoughts are with you. Dear father is away with Uncle Jupp. For this reason I must write in pencil since father has the pen with him. It pleased us to receive your dear letter

Johanna Weisz's Passport Photo.

of 28 October. Praise God that it goes well with you. Remain healthy for us. The sun must shine again for us someday.

Everything has become so different for us. We wait daily for news from the American Consulate that we will be allowed to travel to the United States. Let it be God's will that we obtain entry visas. May the Almighty also bless your good heart, for we know that you do not forget us.

If only dear father could earn something it would not be so difficult. I have written to you how we live. We cannot rent a real apartment, and we are not able to buy [all the new household items we need]. Hopefully we will have the good fortune to come to you soon.

Since 1 November, Uncle B. is also here. He left Berlin four days after us, but as he attempted to cross the border, it was closed, and they did not let him through. Thus, he had to go back to Berlin. A week later he traveled to Dresden and waited there until the border re-opened. Oh my dear Adi, there will be so much to tell you! Unfortunately, while Uncle B. was carrying his heavy trunk, he suffered a hernia, and now that has to heal. This pained us a great deal as well.

Live well my good Adi and take good care. I wish the best in the world for you. Your mother kisses you countless times. Greetings to all dear relatives.

Prague
22 November, 1938
(Heinrich Weisz)

My dear son!

We received your dear letter from the 11th of this month. You write in this letter that you sent ten dollars, but we did not receive the money. Did you send the money separately? It is not clear from your letter. We will wait before writing you and hopefully it will be something good.

We would also like to leave here earlier, but it cannot be arranged. The Czech quota [for visas] is not large and is nearly depleted due to the great demand. As we have already written my dear son, we must sit here and wait.

The situation with work is also bad. Due to the surrendered territories, everything here is overflowing. Free tradesmen, traveling salesmen, and others dare not undertake anything for one year. There are great punishments for infractions. Unfortunately, we are also affected by these measures. Now and then I earn a few Kroner.

Heinrich Weisz's Passport Photo.

The living conditions here are very modest and paltry. The housing conditions are miserable. In order to earn something [and improve this situation], one must be able to speak and write Czech. Mother and I are happy that you do not have to live here. I can make use of my knowledge of Slovak languages. But mother, what do you think? Ernst is already in a Czech school.

Back to the letter in which you write that you can only send us ten dollars. This would be a great help for us. We need a thousand Kroner per month. With ten dollars from you, we have 14 days of our existence. We receive 200 Kroner from the Jewish community, and we run the household very thriftily. In this way, we work through the bad times. Groceries are very primitive and as expensive as in Berlin. Only meat is half the cost. The same is also true of clothes, but naturally, one must have some disposable income. Prague is a very beautiful but old city with many things worth seeing. It is beautiful when one earns money, otherwise everything is worthless. We hope to God for better times and to be together with you my good, dear son.

Be very cautious in your dealings with strange people. In spite of the fact that we worry about you, I know that we can depend on you to take care of things.

Do not forget greetings to the dear aunts, uncles, the girls, and the other young people of Uncle Bennie. In closing dear Adi, we will be glad to be freed from hell, even if we do not have it as good as before. The recent happenings in Germany [*Kristallnacht*] are known to you. Next time I will write a longer letter. For today, be well.

With heartfelt embraces.

Your Papa.

Prague
7 December, 1938
(Johanna Weisz)

My dear golden son!

I have many terms of endearment for you, but I really would prefer to tell them to you in person. Above all else my good Adi, your money has arrived and I thank you wholeheartedly for it. This time you sent it very well. It came through Vienna. We wondered who would send us something from Vienna. We had to go to the customs house where the letter with the American dollars was given to us. We obtained 500 Kroner for the banknote. People who are preparing to emigrate are glad to buy the dollars. Do you see my good boy, your childhood fantasy has become reality. [The reference is unclear.]

My dearest child, just yesterday we received your dear letter of 19 November, which took a considerably long time to reach us. I can figure out to the day when I will receive mail from you. We were very pleased with the letter in that at least we had something to read. We are very thankful that Mr. Weinberg is so friendly to you. Please give him our most heartfelt greetings. Hopefully we will have a chance to get to know him. I am thankful my dear Adi for all the people whom you have gotten to know. You can also be proud of taking the first steps for citizenship.

As I have already written to you, dear father is not allowed to work. You can imagine how very difficult this is for him since father is accustomed to earning money. But working is forbidden by the threat of punishment. I have already written to you my dear child how we live. I console myself with the hope that this is only temporary. Today I will cook a meat-soup, the one that you like so well.

We are very proud of you my dear Adi, and when I speak of you my heart is full. Just last night I saw you in a dream. We are healthy, and praise be to God we will remain so until we receive more good news from you.

Now my dear Adi, I need to ask you if it is possible to procure a winter overcoat in good condition for little Ernst. The one that he obtained from the Jewish community in Berlin is so thin that he freezes in it. Here we cannot buy any such coat [for lack of funds]. And another thing my dear Adi, if you could obtain a suit of clothes for Uncle Adolf, you would bring me great joy. He was so pleased with the top coat that you purchased for him while still in Berlin. You can send these things to our address.

Prague
20 December, 1938
(Heinrich Weisz)

My dear son!

I know that it is not necessary to stress the joy that you have brought to our lives. The good connections that you have established are simply excellent and will certainly be of great use to you. You can imagine how impatient we are to get away from here and to bring some order to our lives. It is simply killing me to be without regular employment for so long.

Dear Adi, I have asked you repeatedly to send me the pictures that you promised. We are very curious to know whether you have changed.

I learned today that dear Paul and Anni, who still live in Budapest, will travel to America in March. This news is very painful because their great fortune [is not ours]. Living in such poor circumstances, we can only console ourselves that we have avoided true hell for the time being. As I have already written to you, the conditions here are meager and only the rich part of the population lives well.

Ernst continues wanting to be your equal. He is growing up nicely and is almost as big as you. With uncle living in the neighborhood, Ernst can play with Erick and Beno [his cousins].

My dear boy, continue along life's path, and with God's help success will be yours. Your dear letters are our only joy. I await your reply to my previous letter. With heartfelt embraces, your ever-loving Papa.

Prague
Late December, 1938
(Johanna Weisz)

My deeply loved, good Adi!

Today we received your dear letter of 3 December with great joy. There was so much news to read that our tea became cold while we read your letter. We are astounded by all the people that you get to know. You are already making your way. I remember how you told us that we should believe in you. [True to your word] you manage well and God will help you with everything. You are our entire ray of hope and we are very proud of you. We still yearn to be with you.

There is still no decision from the American Consulate. We plan to go there ourselves to inquire personally [about the status of our visa application].

My dear son, now that you are so spoiled eating [American food], what will you think of my wretched apricot-noodles? In any event, I am very pleased that your new acquaintances treat you in such a friendly manner. Hopefully we will also get to know them. Life will be beautiful once more when we are joyfully together again.

We are pleased to learn that you will earn more money, and we are curious about your new work. We wish you all imaginable good. Write to us in detail about everything, because even the smallest thing that you do is of great interest to us. We read your dear letters so often that we already know them by heart. We too are pleased by the way that your new acquaintances have taken to you. On your next visit, please give them our warmest regards. Your Aunt Sofie is always amazed when you get to know new people.

Yesterday we lit the first Hanukah candles and Ernst sang. He always speaks a great deal about you. I know that your thoughts are always with us. And so my beloved Adi, we wait longingly for your next letter. Take good care in all that you do. I kiss and embrace you.

Your eternally loving mother.

Many heartfelt greetings and kisses to all dear relatives, especially dear Aunt Sofie and Aunt Rosa.

Prague
Late December, 1938
(Ernst Weisz)

Dear Adi,

I received your lovely card. It pleased me greatly. I would be more glad if I were with you. I am still doing well. Kisses and greetings.

Ernst.

By late November 1938, Heinrich and Johanna Weisz realized that life in Prague was only marginally better than it had been in Berlin, and the outlook for a brighter future was dim. Prevented from securing gainful employment by Czech legislation, Heinrich Weisz competed for low-paying, menial jobs with thousands of other refugees. As a result, the family scraped together a marginal existence. A sparsely furnished one bedroom apartment became home. Meals were irregular and meager. New clothing was a luxury that was out of reach, and entertainment in any form beyond the company of family was not even considered. The "hell" of life in Prague intensified after *Kristallnacht*, the Night of Broken Glass.

During the evening of 9–10 November, 1938, Jews in Germany, Austria, and the Sudetenland were terrorized by Nazi party officials, the SA (Storm Troopers), and their accomplices. Jewish businesses were ransacked, shop windows smashed, and synagogues throughout the Nazi Reich were burned. German citizens joined by looting Jewish stores and passing out "cheap Christmas presents." Neither German police nor fire brigades intervened on behalf of the Jews, and scores were brutally beaten and murdered. When the orgy of violence ended, 91 Jews were dead, 267 synagogues lay in ruins,

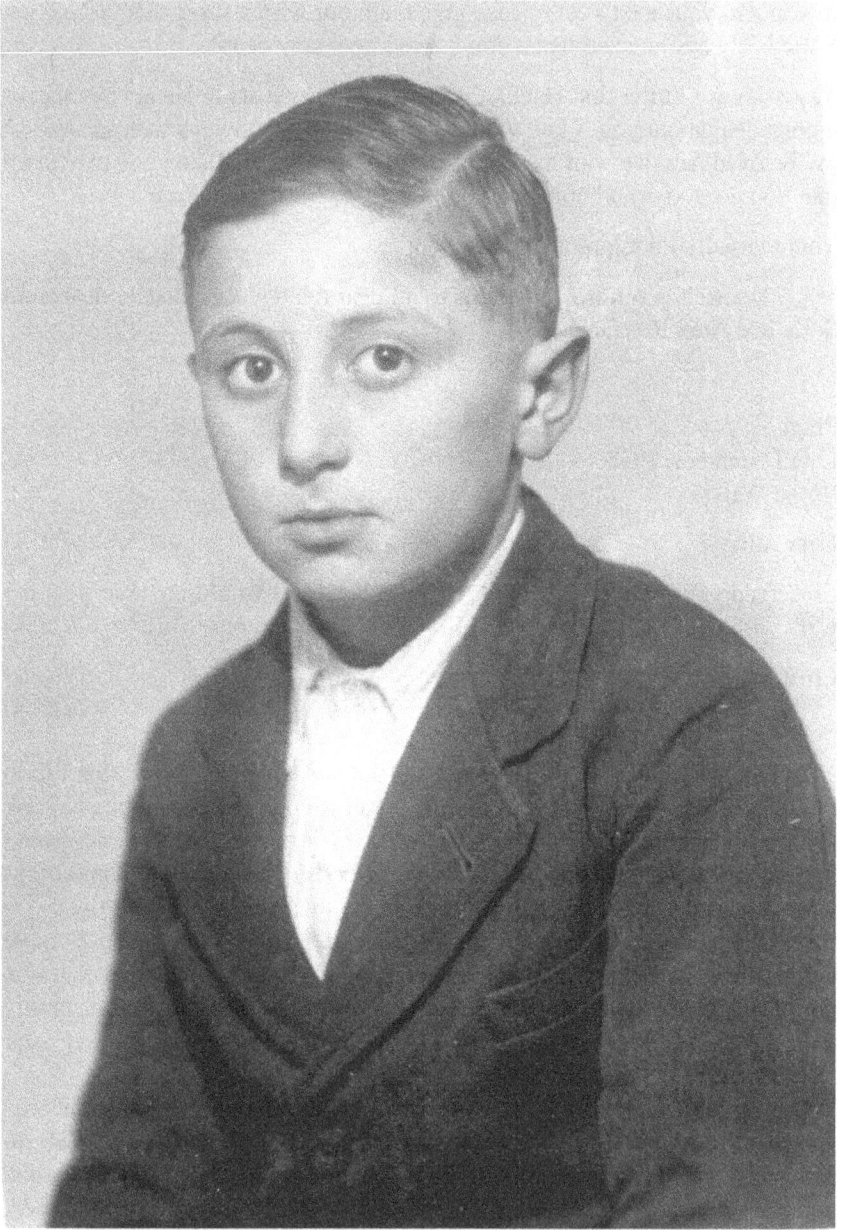

Ernst Weisz's Passport Photo.

7,500 Jewish shops had been vandalized, Jewish cemeteries were desecrated, and 30,000 Jewish men were rounded up and taken to concentration camps at Dachau, Buchenwald, and Sachsenhausen. Even though most of these men were eventually released, an estimated 1,000 Jews died of abuse and torture while in captivity. Those who survived were released after signing a promissory note to leave Germany at the earliest possible moment. While the Nazi propaganda machine and many communal newspapers blamed Jews for inciting the violence, the events of *Kristallnacht* shattered all illusions of a peaceful future for German Jews. According to a local newspaper, "The Jew has played out his hand in Germany."[1]

The violence that rocked German Jewry reverberated throughout the Western world. Daily newspapers in the United States decried the Nazi pogrom as barbaric, unparalleled, and reminiscent of massacres from previous centuries. The European press lambasted the Nazi's treatment of Jews as inhumane and unacceptable. Public protests in European and American cities were organized in support of German Jews. Yet, for all the public protestations, Western governments and Jewish organizations were hesitant to call for sanctions against Germany. Rather, they communicated their displeasure to the Nazi regime through the usual diplomatic channels without demanding that Germany alter its policy toward Jews. The message to both the Nazis and Jews living within the Greater German Reich was clear: the Western world was reluctant to actively intervene on behalf of German Jews. This lesson was not lost on Heinrich and Johanna Weisz who, although spared from the violence, knew that the Nazi storm was gathering strength and threatening Prague. Their increasing anxiety and fear are palpable in their letters to Eddie.

The card from Eddie's brother, Ernst, at the end of 1938 unintentionally belies the strain under which the Weisz family lived since moving to Prague three months earlier. Although they had successfully put breathing space between themselves and the Nazi regime, their living conditions had deteriorated markedly since vacating the family dwelling in Berlin. To make matters worse, government regulations directed against the flood of recent immigrants made it nearly impossible for Heinrich Weisz to contribute to the family's survival. In a particularly poignant letter to his son, Eddie's father lamented that it was simply killing him to be without regular employment for so long. Not only was his family dependent on aid from the Jewish community and cash transfers arranged by Eddie, but Heinrich Weisz became ever more impatient and bitter. He scolded Eddie for not sending the promised photos and reacted bitterly to the news that Paul and Anni in Budapest had secured the coveted visas to migrate to the United States. The meager living conditions and continued delay securing his own travel documents only exacerbated the situation. Moving to Prague meant that Heinrich Weisz was an

unwanted refugee in a foreign land. The once proud patriarch had been completely emasculated. He could do little else but wait impatiently for travel
visas to materialize and experience, vicariously, Eddie's successful transition
to life in the United States.

Unfortunately Johanna Weisz could offer little substantive assistance to her
despondent husband. Having never worked outside of the home and completely unaccustomed to functioning in a foreign language, Johanna Weisz
spent most of her time longing to be reunited with her beloved eldest child.
She lived for his letters and greeted each new one with unabashed joy. While
her husband's work situation clearly troubled her, the separation from Eddie
caused the greatest distress. It was to Eddie that Johanna Weisz turned to for
support, both emotional and material. He was her lifeline, her only hope.

As winter began to exert its hold on central Europe during the final days of
December 1938, Heinrich, Johanna, and Ernst Weisz gathered in their sparsely
furnished and cold one-room apartment to kindle the first Hanukah lights. For
centuries, Jews commemorated the Maccabees' victory over the Seleucid King
of Syria, Antiochus IV, in 165 B.C.E., by lighting candles for eight nights to
symbolize the 'miracle' that occurred when the Temple in Jerusalem was
rededicated. Hanukah was also a time when European Jewish families gathered to eat latkes (potato pancakes) and sufganiyot (jellied filled doughnuts),
and to play dreidel, a four-sided top with letters that stand for the phrase, "a
great miracle happened there." As a child, Eddie looked forward to the yearly
celebration as a time of joy, good food, and special warmth of the family home
resplendent with the Hanukah lights and filled with the aroma of freshly fried
latkes. The memories of a Jewish national resurgence and the accompanying
celebrations contrasted starkly to the reduced circumstances of the Weisz family in 1938. Life under the growing Nazi tempest only allowed for a limited
and somber celebration. Heinrich, Johanna, and Ernst Weisz lit the traditional
lights in December 1938, painfully aware that they had precious little to celebrate. They likely huddled in front of a small menorah, joylessly recited the
Hanukah prayers and songs, and prayed for a miracle that would enable them
to join Eddie in the United States. Perhaps it was this hope that carried them
into the new year and provided them the courage to confront the constant
struggle for survival.

NOTE

1. David Clay Large, *And the World Closed Its Doors. The Story of One Family
Abandoned to the Holocaust,* (New York, Basic Books, 2003), 99.

Chapter Four

Life in Prague

The slow, descending spiral of gloom that cloaked the Weisz family's bleak existence in Prague contrasted starkly to Eddie's blossoming life in the United States. From the moment that he set foot on American soil in June 1938, Eddie immersed himself in the freedom and opportunities of his adopted homeland. After situating himself with relatives and securing employment, he began to explore his new surroundings. During his first few months in America, Eddie frequently rode the busses and subways that connected New York's five boroughs. A five-cent fare paid for journeys that introduced him to the multiethnic metropolis that differed markedly from his native Berlin. Not only did he relish being able to move freely throughout the city, he was enthralled by New York's teeming streets and colorful diversity. On days off, Eddie often spent the afternoon at a Bronx cinema where he soaked up the sights, sounds, and language of his new homeland. The films "Mr. Smith Goes to Washington," starring Jimmie Stuart and Jean Arthur, and "The Adventures of Robin Hood," with Errol Flynn and Olivia de Havilland, served as surrogate language courses for Eddie in 1938. By the time he viewed the 1939 classic "Gone with the Wind," with Clark Gable and Vivien Leigh, he no longer struggled to follow the dialogue. Although Eddie's spoken English remained heavily accented throughout his life, he recalls becoming proficient very quickly. His success as an American and ability to assist his family in Prague depended upon a rapid acculturation process. Time was of the essence for the survival of the entire Weisz clan.

After working in menial labor jobs for a number of months while living in the Bronx near his relatives, Eddie learned about sales opportunities in New York's garment district from an acquaintance he met at one of the weekly dances held at the Empire Hotel on Columbus Circle. In 1938, the Garment

Center was New York's leading industrial center. The sprawling network of factories and clothing stores was located in the middle of Manhattan, between Sixth and Ninth Avenues, from Thirtieth to Forty-Second Streets. The vast majority of ready-made clothing worn by Americans was produced in this area where, each day, thousands of Jewish and Italian immigrants toiled to make new lives for themselves. While working conditions had improved tremendously since the general strikes of 1909–1910 that resulted in legislation against industry sweatshops, garment district workers put in long days of labor pursuing their American dream. For Eddie, selling clothing produced in the garment district provided him an entrée into a new career.

In fall 1938, Eddie moved from the Bronx to Manhattan to take a job as a shipping clerk in a costume jewelry store owned by Yuri Mendrow. While working for Mendrow, Eddie met a man named Eric Kowen who made a living selling men's ties, and he eventually went to work for him during his off hours, peddling ties to clothing stores within the garment district. Eddie received fifty percent of each tie that he sold, and he sent almost all of this money to his family. Obtaining gainful employment proved to be a far simpler task than acquiring the emigration paperwork necessary for his family to leave Prague.

The most important step in the process was securing financial support from someone in the United States willing to sponsor the immigrants. Eddie assumed that Armin Lobl, the maternal uncle who had sponsored his own emigration, would do the same for his parents and brother. According to Eddie, Armin Lobl had the financial resources to extend the aid to his sister and her family. From the time that he arrived in the United States, he spoke frequently with his uncle about the deteriorating situation in Germany for Jews and the urgency of getting his parents out while there was still time. Armin Lobl, however, refused to sign the necessary promissory note. At first he rationalized his decision on the financial uncertainties of the times and the strain of needing to support his sister and brother-in-law should they be unable to secure gainful employment once they arrived in the United States. When Eddie implored his uncle to reconsider and tried to convince him that withholding support jeopardized his sister's life, Lobl claimed that his own wife would not allow him to offer additional support. Eddie's urgent pleas fell on deaf ears, and he was forced to look elsewhere for help. During the final emotional meeting between the two men, Eddie told Armin Lobl before leaving his apartment for the last time, "If I lose my parents, it's your fault." Eddie neither saw nor spoke with his uncle again. The pain and anger of the last encounter with his mother's brother remained raw 65 years later.

Eddie's failure to obtain his uncle's financial assistance proved to be only a momentary setback as he adroitly explored other opportunities for help. During the first few months that he worked for Eric Kowen selling ties, Eddie expanded the goods he sold to include socks and ladies hosiery, a move that helped him develop a large customer base that included both clothing stores and private individuals. Being the personable salesman that he is, Eddie shared his family's plight with many of his customers, a number of whom offered to

Eddie's American Mother, Arlene Schloss.

help. Sometime in mid-1939, a couple by the name of Mr. and Mrs. Schloss befriended Eddie and worked with him to acquire the affidavits. Not only did their help buoy Eddie's spirits, but it provided his family in Prague with renewed hope that they would soon be able to flee Czechoslovakia and rid themselves, once and forever, of the Nazi menace. The correspondence during the first part of 1939 reveals the emotional highs and lows they experienced while trying to secure the necessary paperwork to immigrate to America.

The letters penned by Johanna Weisz in January 1939 reveal the extent to which her life and that of her entire family were intricately intertwined with Eddie's. When reading her letters, one can sense the emotional roller coaster that corresponded to the flow of information between New York and Prague. Each piece of mail lifted Frau Weisz to great heights and kindled moments of hope that allowed her to dream of a brighter future. Comments about housing costs in America and how to furnish a new apartment indicate flashes of optimism in spite of the uncertainties that haunted European Jews in 1939. The lengthy intervals between letters, however, plunged Johanna Weisz back to the reality of her exile in Prague and life on the run from the Nazis. Permanent escape depended upon forces completely out of her control.

Eddie's letters also brought material benefits. Cash, whether sent directly or through an intermediary, was crucial for the family's continued survival. For Eddie, sending the money was the one concrete action he could take to aid his family. He was intensely aware of the increasingly desperate situation faced by European Jews and, in particular, his father's inability to work. The only way he could face the awesome burden with which he was charged when he left Germany 18 months earlier was to send money to his family and remain their beacon for a brighter future. The photos he included in the letters provided tangible evidence of the hope and prosperity that existed for those fortunate enough to gain entry into the United States. Eddie's success at creating an independent life coupled with the strain associated with the effort to rescue his family, were captured in the photographs as well. The photos allowed Johanna Weisz to augment the mental images of Eddie that she carried with her on a daily basis.

Prague
4 January, 1939
(Johanna Weisz)

My lovely good Adi!

We did not receive your lovely letters of 10th and 12th of December until 2 January. We had waited longingly for news from you. There still is no news from the consulate, although we wait daily for it. Our fortune would be great were we with you, if dear father had work and I had my own household. May it be God's will that our desires will soon be fulfilled.

How do things stand with Uncle Armin's request to Sofie [to sign the affidavit of financial support]? I know you made a great effort to get the five dollars from uncle. He has not changed in the least. If only he had a small portion of your goodness, my dear Adi, it would have made my blessed Grandmother very glad. But a good heart must be in a man. I see from your letter that his wife is not much better either. Alas, my dear Adi, do not concern yourself with her.

Yesterday we were with Mrs. Eisler. Although she had offered to send the money to us, we went there in person to retrieve it. You can imagine the joy that it brought us. May God reward you for this and all that you do for us. You are our entire hope.

Mr. Stein has also written to us about the money you sent him. He thinks very highly of you and tells us what a wonderful person you are. It is very nice of you to think of him. He was extremely pleased with your gesture over this, and he wrote to us saying that you are a priceless jewel. Protect your good heart and sunny disposition.

Today, on 4 January, we received your loving letter of 24 December. It took so long to get here. The two pictures that you sent brought mixed emotions. I laughed and cried at them. We looked at them for such a long, long time that your dear face is once again fresh in my memory. You are an artist my dear Adi for having already accomplished so many things.

You certainly remember that Aunt Gitta's nerves were never very strong. At the end of this past November, she had another seizure that was so severe her doctors recommended that uncle bring her to the hospital at (*sic*) Nitra. The seizure is a result of her sorrows. Fortunately, uncle says that she is getting better and will be home in one or two months. It is still very sad and hard on uncle. Throughout the ordeal he must still care for their daughter Rosa, who, in the meantime, has become a young lady. This is quite difficult for uncle.

My dearest child, we wish all the best to the good people who are so kind to you. May you have God's blessing and all imaginable success in your new position.

Your loving Mutti.

Prague
26 January, 1939
(Johanna Weisz)

My dear golden boy!

This time I knew the right day when a letter would come from you. Aunt Rosa was here sharing a cup of tea. Since we live on the ground-floor the mail man only had to knock on the window pane to give me your dear letter. We thoroughly enjoyed your letter and the pictures. As I see from the photo, you have another coat and scarf, but the hat is from home. Your dear, cheerful laugh remains the same, as does your good heart. Be certain that you preserve this for me my good Adi. All things considered, you look wonderful. I believe that you have also matured.

We have already acknowledged the 1,000 Kronen. Ernst is still at school, and he also has boxed a few times with other youngsters. He will not let this activity end. We have also received a letter from Sofie. She travels to Palestine in three weeks with a group. Some wealthy Jewish people provided the money for the trip. Aunt Gitta is besides herself, but Sofie says that she will follow your example dear Adi. She plans to send money to her parents and proposes that they join her later. Hopefully she will keep her word. Uncle Adolf will be glad of this.

We are very glad that you like your new position, and we are certain that you will make your way. We are very fortunate, my dear Adi, that you think only the best for us. Are apartments expensive there? Two rooms will be entirely sufficient for us. And what about the furniture, are the closets built in? We will bring with us our towels, the bedding, and pillows. What do you think, should I bring new pots from here? When I see something special that you would like, I think to myself that I will bring it with me for Adi.

I would like to go to the movies with you. I can imagine how good your English has become. We will learn it as well.

All eyes wait already for the package.

Live well. I kiss you many times. Take care of yourself so that I do not have to worry.

[Your loving Mutti.]

Prague
12 February, 1939
(Heinrich Weisz)

My dear son,

Today is Sunday and, praise be to God, I am back on deck. What I wrote yesterday to you was too little. Although I generally have nothing important to write, I will write a few lines so that you have something to read.

As you can certainly well imagine, we are anxious to leave here as fast as possible. Unfortunately, both I and your dear mother, who misses her familiar household chores, have too much time on our hands. When one cannot be occupied with something enduring or regularly go to the cafe, it is frightfully tedious. Since your dear mother is not inclined to go to the cafes, we sit comfortably at home. When we first arrived, our time was taken up by studying the prices for food and so forth. Today, when this is well known to us, everything is very uninteresting.

One cannot compare the conditions over here with the former ones in Berlin as life is structured completely different. As I already wrote in a letter, food supplies are readily available. Meat, laundry supplies, clothes, and so forth are half the price as in Berlin. But, here there is a crushing unemployment and the employees are paid miserably. Thus, there are employees who hardly earn 800 Kronen [monthly] and occupy a very low level [within society]. The food-stores are open from 6:00 A.M until 8:00 P.M. The cafes, from the simple tavern to the elegant luxury cafes that can hardly be found in Germany, are completely full during the afternoons. It is simply astonishing to see what these people live off of. Apparently there are a great number of idlers. One must be very careful when ordering in the cafes. For example, a cup of coffee is served by two or three waiters, and when one wants a cigar, one must pay a tip. Not much attention is paid to hygiene. For example, anyone can touch the food even if accompanied by a dog. Some things must be accepted as they are. Food and drink are good and not expensive. Butter, eggs, and so forth can be had in abundance. There is also ample fat. And yet, the poor people are in a bad way and the lower echelon employees lead a dog's life. At the same time, there is an upper societal crust that lives better than before.

As a result of the territories surrendered [to the Germans], Prague and the Bohemian lands are very crowded. Thousands of Czechs had to leave the Sudetenland in great haste. In some cases, these people live in barracks. And thus there is political dissatisfaction among the little people. The government issues proclamations in the form of newspaper articles that are without value or usefulness. It is becoming like Germany now. Unfortunately, I also see dark clouds over here as the so-called Jewish question heats up. It will not become as bad as in Jaeckelland [slang term for Germany under the Nazis] because of the democratic Czech population. There is plenty of evidence, however, that a hundred percent democracy is finished. It is fortunate that there are ample food supplies, otherwise the Jew-hunt would already be in motion. Occasionally one sees pasted on placards the words, "Jews out," and so forth. That is how things look here my son. We hope to God that we can leave this home. I could write a great deal more, but I do not want to burden you. You now have an image of what we observe here. Now, write me a detailed letter of your experiences in America and New York.

No more exceptionally private matters for today. Heartfelt greetings and kisses.

Your affectionately loving Papa.

Prague
19 February, 1939
(Johanna Weisz)

My dearest good Adi,

Above all I want to confirm that we received your dear letters of 29 and 31 January. While they were far too short for us, we are pleased to hear from you so punctually. I have also confirmed receiving the check of 28 December.

Uncle Jupp was with us today, Sunday, for dinner. He speaks frequently of you and his concerns. I will distribute evenly the things that you have sent, and Uncle Adolf will receive something as well. As you can imagine, he is in great need of things. You see my dear Adi how much good comes from you.

We still wait daily for news from the consulate. May God provide that soon we all will be together again, and once again I can make dumplings for you. It will also be a great day of joy for us when you will be able to pick us up. We are very proud of you and very happy that you are pleased with your position. Remain healthy and retain your joyful disposition. We are very envious of you. I have shown your picture to many people, and they are amazed at my grown-up son. I tell dear father that no one in the whole world is more devoted than you.

Papa and Ernst are lying down and I will stop soon. When we are together again, you will no longer need an alarm-clock as I will wake you again. Do not go to bed too late my dear young man. Be well my beloved Adi and take care of yourself. I wish you the best of luck and kiss you countless times.

Your affectionately loving Mutti.

Prague
24 February, 1939
(Johanna Weisz)

My beloved good Adi!

All my words are not nearly enough for you. Today is your dear father's birthday. It is still early in the morning and dear father has a few things to attend to before meeting me at the café where I am waiting for him. Without my household or a job, there is nothing I can really do for him. This afternoon we will celebrate at a café. Ernst will be most pleased and will eat three pieces of pie. Naturally I think that this is too much. I would have been especially pleased were we to have received a letter from you today for I know that you would have written about your father's birthday. Hopefully, my good Adi, by the time my next birthday arrives, I will be on the way to you. This would be the most beautiful gift, because I cannot last much longer. I believe I become more impatient when I do not receive mail in a timely manner.

Things are much the same for us. Ernst laughed quite a bit over the fact that you still hold on to your alarm clock from Jaeckelland.

Would it be possible for you to speak earnestly with Eli? He should get his affairs together. To lose so much money. He still thinks that he lives with his parents. Are his professional skills so deficient that he must work in a restaurant? I must honestly say that you are a completely different kind of person. Remain content and prosperous with your work. Your boss's satisfaction and your future are your reward, not to forget, our great joy.

Yesterday we received a letter from Uncle Adolf [in Germany]. Everything with him is the same: he earns little, he has no money, and things have become worse over there. He would like to see us, but that is not possible. When you see Uncle Armin, you can tell him that Uncle Adolf and family might also arrive. Uncle Adolf will write Armin as well.

I will close my writing for today. I kiss all the relatives. To you, my dear good Adi, your loving mother sends heartfelt kisses and greetings. Take heed along your way.

Prague,
24 February, 1939
(Heinrich Weisz)

My beloved young son!

Today on my birthday I find it doubly difficult because you are so far from us, not that I am missing your box of cigars [Eddie's customary gift to his father]. The main thing is that you are always in my thoughts and those of your dear mother. With God's help we will ultimately forsake this place. As you well know, with your help, we do not have tremendous need. We look forward, however, to being with you and finally having our feet on solid ground. Time does not stand still, and we hope for the best. My greatest desire is to be with you, and I would love to be present at your very successful boxing matches. It is clear that your size has increased, and before long you will be fighting as a heavyweight. Ernst sends his congratulations, and therefore I do not have to do so.

It pleases me that you are making such good progress and already stand on your feet. You are not dependent on anyone. You have become a man. I do not have to tell you that I and others admire you.

Now, my dear good son, remain as you are so that we will share many joys together. More in my next letter. For today, your tenderly-loving father sends his heartfelt greetings and kisses.

Prague
2 March, 1939
(Johanna Weisz)

My beloved good Adi!

Once again your letter arrived on the day I calculated it would. Even though you could not arrange otherwise and it arrived two days after father's birthday, we were very happy [to hear from you]. It is always a holiday for us when we receive your letters. It would really be nice to have more pictures from you.

Ernst boxes regularly with other youngsters. I am always admonishing him not to fight so often, but the fighting is practically a daily occurrence. His fingers are quite banged up. He makes good progress and is very proud of you. Presently he thinks that he is ready to live alone with you and help us in this way.

This year, dear Papa truly missed your birthday-cigars. Hopefully, the next celebration will be much nicer.

The rents here are very expensive, but with God's help in reuniting us with you, a large room will be enough. Do you think that I should bring things like kitchen pots with me? What does a salt shaker cost [in America]? We are currently taking English classes again because without a language, one has no chance; but with it, one progresses more rapidly.

My dear Adi, do not worry about us. We have what we need to eat and drink, and with your help everything will turn out well. Many are envious because of the support that you provide us.

Ernst was angry that you did not write him. What do you think about his drawings? When we last inquired at the consulate, we were told that we still will have to wait for half a year. The crush [to leave Prague] is very great. We only need to remain healthy, and then things will be good for us again.

Be well my dear Adi. Take heed along your way. I kiss you warmly.

Your affectionately loving Mutti.

Prague
2 March, 1939
(Heinrich Weisz)

My dear young man,

There is only a little space left for me. I am thankful for your birthday wishes and the usual cigars can wait until next time. Naturally you mean much more to me than everything in the world.

Dear mama looks fine, as does the little boxer. I am tired today, and this is why I have so little to write. Next time I will have five times as much to write. Yes, I am tired and perhaps will do nothing. I am conserving my strength for when I am over there with you.

It is 9:30 and I must go to bed. Good night my boy. Greetings and countless kisses. Your deeply beloved Papa.

Write to our new address. From 15 March we will be living at Prague, I Karlova 24. 1.

Prague
10 March, 1939
(Johanna Weisz)

My dearest, best Adi!

The rain drops knocking on my window bring greetings from you. This is actually what happened. When the postman gave me your dear letter through the window, it was raining. In the future this will no longer be the case since we are changing apartments and will be living in an upstairs unit. I am already looking forward to the move and will describe the apartment for you.

Ernst has a small 'chamber-maid's' room like we had for you. There is a bed and an armoire. In our room, there is a small oven where I can cook. [The apartment] costs us 350 Kronen per month. Thanks to your help and that which we receive from the [Jewish] community, we can afford it.

I must tell you that we have no worries over here. The only thing is that we long for you. When we are all together, life will be beautiful for us again.

Prague
Sometime in late February 1939 or early March
(Ernst Weisz)

Dear brother Adi!

I received your beautiful card and it pleased me greatly. I already have 64 cards in my album, eleven of which are cards from you from beautiful America. I am learning well at school. In writing I received 2 ones, 6 twos, and a 3. But everything is written in Czech. In Arithmetic, 2 threes and a two. In Homework, a two and a half, and a three. In Dictation, a two and a three.

We are moving to a better apartment on March 15, and I will go to another school. Our new address is Karlova 24, Patno 1. I also have a pretty girlfriend. I get together with her often. I could not write about this in my previous letter because I had no time. But today I write more.

Everyday I wonder what you will send me. I can hardly wait for this, and I think of it all the time. Now I close for today. Greetings and kisses to all. Give my greeting to Elias.

Your brother Ernst.

On 12 February, 1939, shortly before his 59th birthday, Heinrich Weisz penned a strikingly poignant letter to his eldest son that depicted an existence riddled by dualities. The opening comment about being "back on deck" suggests a recent recovery from what may well have been a bout of depression. A circumscribed life accentuated by Heinrich Weisz's inability to work or provide for his family shattered his self image, and his outlook clearly vacillated between despair for the present and hope for the future. The lack of work and a structured routine also resulted in a monotonous existence that was only broken with letters from Eddie. News of their son's successful integration into American life buoyed Heinrich and Johanna Weisz's spirits more than anything else. A stark portrait of a divided Czech society was also drawn. While the wealthy spent idyllic afternoons in Prague's luxurious cafes enjoying fine coffees, pastries, and cigars, the poor lived a crushing existence. Their meager incomes placed the bountiful foodstuffs available in city grocery stores out of reach. Although depravation and hunger had yet to seize the Czech capital and a diminished democratic government remained in power for the time being, Heinrich Weisz feared that deteriorating conditions would exacerbate the situation for Jews. Nevertheless, in February 1939, Prague was a more hospitable place for Jews than Berlin.

Johanna Weisz still clung tenaciously to the lifeline provided by Eddie's letters. Almost every letter she wrote reviewed the status of her correspondence with Eddie and descriptions of her attachment to each one. Her moods clearly rose and fell with the arrival of mail from the United States, and news from Eddie remained her stabilizing anchor when faced with the reduced circumstances of life in Prague. The anticipated celebration of Heinrich Weisz's birthday is described with an air of resignation due to the lack of financial resources and a fully equipped kitchen in which she could prepare a proper celebratory meal. Much like her husband, Johanna Weisz had lost the means to fulfill her life's role. The proud homemaker's only solace was her absent son's accomplishments. As life's deteriorating circumstances continued to close in on Johanna Weisz, she focused intently on a forthcoming reunion with Eddie.

The letters written by Johanna, Heinrich, and Ernst Weisz in March 1939, offer little evidence of the chaotic situation in which they lived. The fixation on post from Eddie remained constant as family members went about their daily routines. For Ernst, this involved school, boxing, and time spent with his girlfriend, typical activities for a 12-year-old boy. His letter's matter-of-fact tone, coupled with his mother's remarks about Ernst's desire to assist the family, reveal the steady maturation of a boy who lived under the darkening cloud of Nazism. Ernst Weisz hoped that he would soon join his brother in 'beautiful' America. Johanna Weisz also spent a great deal of time preparing for life across the Atlantic. She contemplated how best to equip her new kitchen and took English lessons to help ease the eventual transition. These mental exercises enabled her to remain stoically optimistic about the future. In the meantime, she also looked forward to a new apartment in Prague, one that provided a bit more personal space for the entire family. Financial support from Eddie and the Prague Jewish community maintained a relatively secure existence for the Weisz family, albeit in circumstances greatly reduced from what they had been before the Nazi seizure of power. So long as the Weisz family lived in the Czechoslovakian democracy, they did not fear for their lives. The events of March 15, however, dramatically altered their outlook and accentuated their desire to flee Europe.

Chapter Five

The Return of the Jackal

The Weisz family's move to Prague in September 1938 provided them a momentary respite from their Nazi persecutors. Deprived of citizenship and the opportunity to work in Germany, Heinrich, Johanna, and Ernst Weisz hoped to make Prague a temporary haven while they arranged to immigrate to the United States. Even when the western portions of Czechoslovakia known as the Sudetenland were ceded to Germany, and Prague was inundated with refugees fleeing the Nazis, Jewish inhabitants of the famed city were not harassed or physically threatened. Although a far cry from life in Germany before the Nazis seized power in January 1933, Prague was a welcome sanctuary for the Weisz family and the 56,000 Jews who called it home. This situation changed dramatically on March 15, 1939.

When the British and French ceded the Sudetenland to Germany in September 1938, Hitler assured Prime Ministers Neville Chamberlain and Edouard Daladier that he was a man of peace and would demand nothing else from his neighbors. Yet, less than six months later, Hitler reneged on his word and ordered German troops to occupy all of Bohemia and Moravia. In short order, an independent Czechoslovakia ceased to exist, and in its place the Nazis created the Protectorate of Bohemia and Moravia. The newly established political entity was ruled by the Nazis, although the last president of Czechoslovakia, Emil Hácha, retained the title of State President. The remaining Czechoslovakian territory of Slovakia, located to the east of Bohemia and Moravia, became a client state of the Nazis under the leadership of the Catholic priest and politician Jozef Tiso.

Following the dismemberment of Czechoslovakia, the Nazis quickly assumed control of the civil bureaucracy. Within days, Nuremberg-style laws deprived Jews of their civil service positions and citizenship. Foreign-born

Jews, like the Weisz family, were particularly vulnerable. The Protectorate's Gentile population was also affected by the Nazi takeover. Czech citizens were requisitioned to work in coal mines, the iron and steel industry, armaments production, and thousands were sent to Germany to work as forced laborers. Strict rationing was imposed on the entire Czech population, and the once abundant consumer goods became increasingly scarce. The days of a tenuous, albeit short-lived, reprieve for the Weisz family were over. The German Jackal had cornered Heinrich, Johanna, and Ernst Weisz once again. This precarious situation was not lost upon Eddie who worked frantically to expedite his family's emigration.

When news of Czechoslovakia's collapse reached Eddie, he was living in New York's Manhattan borough, selling ties, ladies' stockings, and other articles of clothing. In spite of working long hours, Eddie took home an average of $10 per week, an amount far too little to sponsor his family's emigration. After paying $3 per week for his room and buying food, Eddie set aside what he could to send to his family. The financial affidavits of support necessary to secure the immigration papers would have to be provided by an individual with greater capital than Eddie could acquire. Upon arriving in the United States, Eddie naively assumed that his mother's brother, Armin Lobl, would come to the aid of his family. When his uncle refused to sign the necessary financial affidavits, Eddie turned to his clients for help. Amazingly, a number of people whom he had met while working his sales beat volunteered to write letters on behalf of his family. Before the Nazis had occupied Prague, the president of the S.M. Franken pipe company, Herbert Schloss, wrote affidavits for the Weisz family and pledged to support them financially should they not be able to secure adequate work after they arrived in the United States. Upon receiving the cherished affidavits, Heinrich and Johanna Weisz filed them with the American embassy in Prague and secured their passport pictures. Tragically, however, the papers were lost when the United States relocated its Prague embassy staff to Vienna after March 15, 1939, and the process of securing the necessary paperwork had to begin anew. The increasing frustration and concern are captured in the correspondence that followed the Nazis' occupation of Prague.

Interestingly, however, the letters do not comment initially about the changed political situation in Prague. Heinrich Weisz did not write about the torching of a synagogue in Vsetin or that 118,310 individuals living in the Protectorate were designated as Jews according to the Nuremberg Laws, even though only 86,715 were members of the local Jewish communities. Most likely, Eddie's father was concerned about German censors and felt it prudent to limit the letter to banal family matters. Yet, the first letter sent immediately following the Nazi's complete dismemberment of Czechoslovakia reveals a high level of anxiety, and the Passover themes that resonate throughout would not be lost on Eddie. The opening passage comments that "it would be enough" for Eddie to write punctually, a reference to the traditional "Dayenu" sung at Passover tables throughout the world. The Hebrew lyrics mean that if He (God) had only brought the Jews out of Egypt it would have been enough. The second verse adds that if He had only given the Torah of Truth, it would have been enough. If only Eddie would write often, it would be enough for his parents. The Passover theme is also present when Heinrich Weisz comments about celebrating Passover together next year in New York. The concluding words of each Seder meal held outside of Israel are "Next Year in Jerusalem." Not only does Eddie's father refer to next year in New York, he employs the Hebrew word for year, *Shanah*, as opposed to the German word, *Jahr*. The themes of deliverance and freedom from slavery that are central to the celebration of Passover are embedded in this letter. Heinrich Weisz prays for deliverance from his Nazi oppressor. In the meantime, he lives for news from his son, and the money that he sends is key to his family's survival.

Prague
2 April, 1939
(Heinrich Weisz)

My dearest young man!

After four weeks [of not hearing from you], we finally received your dear letter and postcard. You can imagine how impatient we get. We thank God that we are healthy, and we are only pleased when we have mail from you. There is no need to always write something lengthy. It is enough to punctually receive mail from you.

The weather has been very cloudy lately, and it has rained quite a bit. Tomorrow is Pesach but, unfortunately, without you. We have invited Uncle Jojo. Hopefully, next year we will be with you in New York.

How are you getting along with your work? It pleases me that you, my child, are firmly established. That remains for us our great hope.

Have you finally sent the package? If not, please send it promptly because I definitely will have no rest from Uncle Jojo until the package arrives. Tomorrow I will seek out Mrs. Eisler in order to retrieve your greetings. I always rejoice greatly over that. We will then communicate more specifically what she has to tell.

Write me and let me know if and where you have been invited for the holiday. We have one wish, to get away from here and be with you soon. How long do we have to wait? We have to console ourselves that also this time will arrive. As you well know from Uncle Sami's brother, their entire family has traveled to Palestine to wait for the time over there. May God grant that they are successful, because they have traveled illegally by steamboat. We still do not know when the others will travel.

Live well my good boy. With heartfelt kisses,

Your loving Papa.

Prague
9 April, 1939
(Johanna Weisz)

My dear Young one!

We received your two dear letters together with a postcard for young Ernst.

In the meantime, no doubt you also must have received a letter from us. All things considered, praised be God that we are healthy.

It is not necessary for Uncle Band to come at the present time since we have recently been invited three times. We were very pleased by invitations.

Now my dear Adi, it falls very heavily upon me, your beloved mother, to inform you of the following. Once again we were at the American Consulate where we were told the depressing information that we will have to wait a very, very long time for our departure. They estimated that it would be approximately three years before we could travel. You can imagine our upset, especially since good [legal] advice is very expensive. Even though it is possible to get away from here through other means, this path is unfortunately closed to us. We cannot obtain a visa for either France or Holland because there is no one over there that can vouch for us. We also tried to drop in at the English Consulate, but the crowd was so great that it was impossible to even get close. We had been told that we might obtain a visa for England, if we could produce a cash payment or if someone else could make a deposit on our behalf. Uncle Bernat is also affected by the same situation.

Now my child, please be so good and inquire at the English Consulate about how we might proceed. Perhaps you will succeed in moving the brother of dear Sami for this purpose or even someone else. You know that the money is guaranteed. In the meantime, we will certainly carry on, and basically it is a mere charity-service for us. At the consulate you must proceed on our behalf, acting as if we were there ourselves to provide the necessary deposit. Otherwise, we will not obtain the visa.

Perhaps you have other information from HIAS [Hebrew Immigrant Aid Society] that will be better for us. How much easier things would be if HIAS were here! Yes, first off to HIAS.

Mutti

Johanna Weisz's fear and confusion are palpable. On one hand, she communicated to Eddie that there was no need for "Uncle Band" to visit. Band was the Czech ex-patriot who released money from his Prague bank account to the Weisz family in exchange for dollars he received from Eddie. The three visits refer to multiple denominations of currency they received. (Eddie is no longer certain whether it was three hundred or three thousand Krone). When the Nazis moved into Prague in March 1939, Mr. Band instructed his bank to release all of his remaining funds to Eddie's parents. In spite of their relatively fluid cash position, the situation had become desperate.

The chaotic scene that enveloped the American Consulate in Prague following the March 15 invasion is not difficult to imagine. Panicked Jews, desperate to escape their Nazi pursuers, mobbed the embassy to beseech American officials for exit visas. Yet, as is now well documented, consulate officials had been instructed to delay, by any tactics possible, granting emigration paperwork to Jews. A concerted effort by the United States Department of State to prevent Jewish refugees from reaching America resulted in Heinrich and Johanna Weisz being told that it would be three years before their visas would be granted. With the German Jackal bearing down on them, they grasped for an escape route. The shred of news on which they hung their hope was word that England was granting visas to Jews with the financial wherewithal to make an immediate cash deposit. Moving from the American Consulate, where their plans to join Eddie in New York had been shattered by heartless bureaucrats, to a panicked mob that engulfed the British government offices, Heinrich and Johanna Weisz had no option but to implore Eddie to act on their behalf. If the rumors were true, maybe it would be possible for Eddie to navigate the bureaucratic maze from the relative calm that prevailed within the United States. Perhaps, Frau Weisz communicated to Eddie, the Hebrew Immigrant Aid Society could assist them. After all, they were in the business of helping Jews. The tragedy, of course, is that the goodwill and Herculean efforts of aid workers and relatives such as Eddie was no match for the determined efforts of government officials to prevent, for as long as necessary, the influx of Jewish refugees into the United States and England. Naively oblivious to the futility of their endeavors, the entire Weisz clan redoubled its efforts. Letters to Eddie in the subsequent months were more sporadic than they had been since his family moved to Prague, and they offer glimpses into the increasingly anxious situation in which they lived.

Prague
30 May, 1939
(Johanna Weisz)

My darling good Adi!

I was very concerned that I did not receive mail from you on my birthday. Since your departure and our separation, I am no longer able to rest when two weeks pass without news from you. I rejoiced when your dear letter [finally] arrived, and I even cried. May God grant that we are with you next May 15th [my birthday]. I have so many wishes my good Adi, and I must take your word that everything will work out.

It is such beautiful weather today. We are sitting here at a concert. I have drunk a coffee, Papa has a glass of beer in front of him and the accompanying cigar. Young Ernst has already eaten a large dish of potato salad that I made. He really enjoyed the lovely card that you sent him, my dear Adi. He looks to you as an example in all that he does.

Unfortunately, we still have no decision from the consulate. How happy I would be if once again I had a small household to manage and knew that my larger one would return to me one day. This would be such a lovely development. I hope that in July we will be called to the consulate; then we will learn how long the wait will be.

By the time you receive this letter, your vacation will be over. I wish that you will have had a good rest because I know that you work hard. It is very nice of your boss to pay for a week's vacation. I wish you such luck with all people you meet. You deserve it, my dear Adi. Last night I dreamt that I kissed you.

I will stop for today my dear Adi. Remain healthy for me, and I beg you, take heed along your way. I kiss you many times.

Your tenderly loving Mutti.

Prague
30 May, 1939
(Heinrich Weisz)

My dear young man,

Do me a singular pleasure and write at least one postcard every week. Your dear mother is miserable when she does not receive a letter from you every 8 days.

My good son, I take great pleasure and praise God that you are so industrious. The one wish that I have for myself is that with God's help we would all be together. This will be the most beautiful day of my life.

We are still learning English so that we, God willing, will at least be able to make ourselves understood and be employed.

Young Ernst is also an entirely good child. He was very pleased with your card. Be good my son, and send us the promised pictures. Over here it is already summer, and hopefully this time will also pass. Young Ernst longs for you.

There is a large clock in the area which gives the time here and in New York. Your dear mother and young Ernst go there often and speak of you and what you are doing at that moment.

All things considered my dear son, things are well with us, although unfortunately we are at a great distance from you. We are healthy, and with your help, we have what we need. I could write to you like this for hours, but I always must leave something for next time. Now, my good son, I send you my heartfelt greetings and embraces.

Your tenderly loving Papa.

Prague
30 May, 1939
(Ernst Weisz)

I was pleased to receive your card. Thank you for your good wishes. You will be my model. Dear mother was very concerned that you do not write often. We really like having letters from you. Especially dear mama!

As soon as it gets warm I will learn how to swim. I am getting a new swimsuit from Papa!

Many greetings and kisses.

Ernst

Our address: Prague V. Meiselova 3 II.b. Kaprosova (Father's handwriting)

Prague
15 August, 1939
(Heinrich Weisz)

My dear son!

I write to you today from outside of the Reich. It is very difficult to become accustomed to treachery [of the current situation]. This letter contains our new address. Write to us soon, for we do not know how long we will be able to stay in this new apartment. It is very difficult for us to find an appropriate apartment since not everyone wants to rent to a married couple with a child. It is also difficult to find accommodations with cooking facilities. We will easily overcome these obstacles, however, since praise God, all of us are in good health. Ultimately this is the main thing.

We are pursuing all possibilities to get out of here as quickly as possible. A woman recently gave us advice that will perhaps help. She told me that you should contact [the consulate] in Washington and arrange for us to be placed on the quick-list, the top priority-quota, so that we will not have to wait so long. You must make the request in the following manner. You will need your affidavit and the one from the sisters and for us to be placed on the priority-list. I wait for your letter, hoping to hear from you soon. Once I hear from you, I will respond immediately. So my dear boy, let's see how you manage this task.

There is nothing in particular for today. Thousands of greetings and kisses.

Your ever loving-you Papa.

Our new address is Prague-Smichow Smetanova ul 1.111.

Prague
23 August, 1939
(Heinrich Weisz)

My dear son,

When this letter is in your hands, we will already be living in our new quarters [apartment]. We had to change yet again. We would be very happy if we were able to settle outside of Europe. I feel fortunate that you have been spared all of this. Praise God.

We do not have any reliable information about our Italian trip. We do not know when we could leave or what we will be over there. We must reconsider everything. The eternal waiting plays on one's nerves. My dear son, everything comes to an end, and I think that the time will come when we are together again.

Write and let me know how you have managed in regards to the priority affidavit.

It certainly cannot disrupt things if we were to have some good luck.

We are making difficult progress with our English lessons since we have to think about all sorts of other things. We are in the seventh level. Dear Mama is more diligent than I, as she would like to arrive in the United States as a complete Englishwoman.

All things considered, my dear son, things are not so bad. We have what we need. Do not send anything since Herr Jackal will nibble on it all. He is always hungry and this makes me fearful.

Do not forget to give both aunts hearty greetings from us. Many, many hearty greetings and kisses to you, my dear son.

Your loving Papa.

Prague
26 September, 1939
(Johanna Weisz)

My dearly beloved Adi!

In this exceedingly difficult time, all my thoughts are still with you. We know how ardently you are waiting for us. When I woke today, you were once again my first thought. It is your birthday, the second time without us. My beloved Adi, I wish you every imaginable good. I pray that God will allow you to be happy and well. Always remain healthy for me, and may you encounter only good things along your way.

We were deeply concerned that so long had passed without a letter. Today, after five weeks, your dear letter finally arrived, and we were greatly relieved. You are right my son that we must keep our nerves. May God soon grant us the passionately desired peace that will come when we see one another again. We are healthy, and we have what we need to eat. If only we had luck with the priority visa and the American Consulate. You see how frighteningly slow that goes.

The High Holidays [Rosh Ha Shanah and Yom Kippur] were also very sad for us. While they were not very festive last year, they were entirely miserable this year. It would be splendid to be with you and to be relieved from all that oppresses me. We would have so many, many things to say to each other.

We will move once more on October 1 into our own small apartment. This will be much better and it is near your aunt.

Now my dear Adi, remain healthy. Do me a favor and take heed along your way so that I will not worry so. I hope that your birthday was enjoyable. I kiss you heartily.

Your loving Mutti.

Our new address: Prague XVI Na-Elni 6

Eddie circa 1939.

The letters sent to Eddie at the end of May 1939, marked a full year since he left Germany for the United States. His family, however, made no reference to this anniversary. All three letters comment about the lack of regular mail from Eddie and the impact that this had on Johanna Weisz. One senses the utter disappointment and despair that took hold when she did not receive birthday greetings from Eddie on her birthday. Frau Weisz laments at being separated from Eddie and the need to hear regularly from him; Heinrich Weisz implores his son to write at least "every eight days," and even young Ernst tells his older brother to write more often. Yet, the lack of frequent correspondence did not result from Eddie failing to write regularly. He recalls sending letters once a week. One can only assume that postal service delays and disruptions were common in Nazi-controlled Europe, a situation that accentuated the powerlessness of Jews living under German control. Without a household from which to operate and separated from her oldest son, Johanna Weisz was adrift. Letters from Eddie functioned as an anchor that prevented her from plunging into the depths of depression.

The letters also do not refer to Ernst's 13th birthday having passed without celebrating his Bar Mitzvah, the ceremony for Jewish boys marking their transition to adulthood. Eddie's Bar Mitzvah in 1930 was a grand celebration attended by friends and family, including his Uncle Armin Lobl from the United States. After Eddie was called to the Torah to recite a blessing and chant the *Maftir*, the section of the weekly Torah portion sung by the Bar Mitzvah, the Weisz family celebrated their son's coming of age with a sumptuous meal. What had been a festive celebration for Eddie was not to be for Ernst. The entire Weisz family had to have been acutely aware of their inability to celebrate Ernst's Bar Mitzvah, even though they do not mention it in their letters. Rather than dwelling on their reduced circumstances, the correspondence focuses on their daily routines, the frustrations of waiting to hear from the American Consulate, and Eddie's life in America. Perhaps this is one reason that all three letters refer to Eddie being a role model for Ernst. The Weisz family could only hope that Ernst would have the opportunity to emulate his older brother's success. Ernst's opportunities, however, were determined by a completely different set of circumstances than those experienced by Eddie growing up in Weimar, Germany. The world had changed dramatically in a few short years, and conditions for European Jews grew increasingly perilous with each passing month.

By summer's end in 1939, the Nazis were bearing down on Prague's Jewish community. The combination of German pressure and a growing local anti-Jewish movement led to increased discrimination against Jews and outright persecution. The Jewish synagogue in Vsetin was torched on March 15, 1939, the day that the Nazis occupied Prague. On July 27, 1939, Adolf Eichmann, the Nazi's 'logistics' officer for the Jews in Europe, established a branch of the Central Office for Jewish Emigration in Prague. This bureaucracy required Jews to register for emigration, divested them of most of their property, and coordinated the exclusion of Jews from all aspects of Prague's economic, cultural, and political life. The Weisz family's inability to secure adequate housing and need to move repeatedly stemmed directly from these developments. The situation became more treacherous with each passing day, a fact that caused Heinrich and Johanna Weisz to grasp at every perceived opportunity for escape. From their desire to secure a "top priority quota" to vacating Prague for Italy, they were desperate to leave. Heinrich Weisz fear of "Herr Jackal" was palpable.

The deteriorating living conditions hit Johanna Weisz particularly hard, and she was propelled to new emotional lows during the Jewish High Holy Days of Rosh Ha Shanah and Yom Kippur. What was meant to be a time of reflection and renewal devolved into a "miserable" experience for Johanna Weisz. Separated from her beloved eldest son and deprived of a home from which she could care for her family, Johanna Weisz clung tenaciously to Eddie's lifeline. Her safety, and that of her family, depended on his ability to secure the necessary paperwork. With the outbreak of war in September 1939, however, immigration possibilities narrowed precipitously. Not only did the United States drastically limit the number of European Jews who could enter the country, but Nazi officials were formulating a new solution to the "Jewish Problem." The Jackal was circling its prey, gradually closing off all avenues for escape. The coming months would prove determinate for the entire Weisz clan.

Chapter Six

War in Europe

When German Panzer divisions stormed into Poland on September 1, 1939, the *New York Times* carried the following headline: "German Army Attacks Poland; Cities Bombed, Ports Blockaded; Danzig is Accepted into the Reich." The entire front page was filled with stories about the hostilities and the political fallout. Dramatic full-page headlines continued for seven days, and the front sections remained chocked full of details about the intense diplomatic maneuvers that reverberated throughout Europe and beyond. The *Times* even ran a story about Mayor Fiorello LaGuardia's press conference at which he announced the actions taken by the city to prepare for "any war emergency." Yet, apart from the attention given to the war in the local media and the traffic jams in Times Square as people slowed to read the latest headlines, New York City remained largely unaffected by events across the Atlantic Ocean. Movie houses ran their regular schedule of feature films. ("Goodbye Mr. Chips," "The Wizard of Oz," and Carole Lombard and Cary Grant's "In Name Only" were playing during the first week of September.) New York sports fans reveled in the Yankees 12-game lead over their division rivals, the Boston Red Sox, and the horse racing season continued without interruption at Saratoga. Interestingly, the one place that seemed to embody New Yorkers' collective anxiety was the World's Fair, an international extravaganza that had opened earlier in the year. On Saturday, September 2, the Times declared that the Fair had become a "microcosm of war fears and hopes."

Plans for the New York World's Fair were hatched in 1935 by a group of business men and politicians interested in jump starting New York's economy. Led by Grover Whalen, the New York World's Fair Corporation spent $157,000,000 to create a vast complex of more than 200 buildings, 62 miles of roads, 10,000 trees, and two million shrubs that were situated on 1,200 acres of a converted ash dump in Queen's Flushing Meadows. Participants at the Fair included 58 nations, two international organizations, 33 states, 76 concessionaires and 1,354 exhibitors. "The World of Tomorrow," as the Fair was called, opened to the public on April 30, 1939, with a presentation by President Roosevelt, and 198,791 people poured through the turnstiles that day. Admission cost 75 cents for adults and 25 cents for children ages 3 to 14. Although the Fair was open daily throughout the summer from 9:00 A.M. until 2:00 A.M. and, in spite of the aggressive marketing by Whalen and Mayor LaGuardia, attendance figures never reached their expected levels.

With the outbreak of war in September, officials associated with the Fair worked furiously to preserve its international character. All government exhibits remained open until the Fair closed for the winter on October 31, 1939. When the Fair re-opened in May, 1940, the pavilion sponsored by the Soviet Union was gone and many of the sites hosted by European countries were scaled down and restructured to include references to the war. Although the Fair remained open throughout the summer in 1940, it never recaptured the spirit and energy of its first year. Most Americans were more concerned about the possibility of war than they were about the prospects for a distant future. This transformation and the events they represented are evident in Eddie's life and his family's deteriorating situation.

The outbreak of war in Europe did little to interrupt Eddie's busy schedule. In addition to working for Mendel's jewelry store and selling clothing on the side, he worked as a physical trainer at the Young Men's Hebrew Association (YMHA) located on Lexington Avenue. Having been an avid boxer who competed regularly while in Germany, Eddie joined the YMHA to maintain his boxing skills. Within a few months after joining the YMHA, Eddie's boxing prowess and athletically sculpted physique became well known at the local "Y," and he was solicited to personally train individuals interested in honing their talents. One of his clients was a man by the name of Lobe, whose father was the president of the company that produced Brillo Scouring Pads. Before long, Eddie and his client became friends, and the two men often dined at the Lobes' home. One evening in the fall of 1939, while dining at the Lobe residence, Mr. Lobe told Eddie of a sales opening that he had in Detroit and inquired whether Eddie would be interested in working for him. Although pleased at the opportunity and potential increase in pay, Eddie had one concern: he did not know where Detroit was. Anxious to hide his enthusiasm but not afraid to reveal a profound lack of familiarity with U.S. geography, Eddie politely asked Mr. Lobe if Detroit was in America. When the Lobe family realized that Eddie was sincere, they retrieved an atlas from their bookshelves and gave Eddie an impromptu geography lesson. A few months later, Eddie moved to Detroit to assume a job selling Brillo Scouring Pads. Before relocating to Detroit at the end of 1939, letters from Eddie's family slowed on account of the war. Their content, however, reveals a stark contrast between Eddie's good fortune and their own difficulties.

Eddie in Detroit.

Prague
11 October, 1939
(Heinrich Weisz)

My dear young man!

I can understand your concern about us, but it is entirely unfounded. Thanks be to God we have everything we need. In this respect, you can be certain. We hope that there will soon be peace in the world so that we will be able to continue our journey. We have not received any information from the American Consulate, and you can hardly imagine how slowly they work. We have to keep our nerve, remain patient, and bide our time. In any event, there is nothing that can be done. With time comes counsel. These difficult times will also pass.

It was proper for you to go to Temple, and it would make me very happy to pray and sing with you as I used to do regularly.

The fact that our apartment is in the same city district as Uncle Bernhard's reduces our boredom and is also very beneficial for young Ernst. And so my good son, you see that it is possible for one to slowly get used to everything. Our thoughts are with you daily.

How are things with Aunt Sofie and Rosa and with dear Helen in her young marriage? Write to me about everything because all that you do is of interest to me. How are things with your training? Is the Maccabee Club in full swing? I could go on asking you questions, but I will leave some things for the next letter. I will now stop for today and close with thousands of greetings and kisses for you, my Eddie. Give my regards to the dear aunts and Eli.

Affectionately yours, Papa.

Address: Prague-Smichov, Na Clene 6. II

Prague
8 November, 1939
(Johanna Weisz)

My sincerely beloved good Eddie,

It was only yesterday, after five long weeks, that we received your loving letter of 1 October. We thoroughly enjoyed your dear letter and the beautiful picture, although I cried at seeing how much taller and stronger you have grown. We wish you all the best. You are still our only hope. Our health remains good, and we have everything we need.

Uncle Jupp was with us this evening for a meal of goulash. He visits often, and on Sundays, I always cook for him. It pains me to see him so lonely, but he says that as long as we are here he knows where to go.

It is already 10:00 P.M. and young Ernst is asleep. He learns well at school and his Czech is quite good. Our current little apartment consists of a room and a kitchen. I acquired some nice kitchen furnishings from a lady who left the building. We only need to remain healthy until the time comes when, with God's help, we will see one another again.

Our neighbors are Czech, and they are very decent and helpful people. They are with us almost every evening.

I am getting tired now and should go to bed. My dear Eddie, you are my last thought before falling asleep each night. Be well my good boy.

Farewell and kisses from your loving Mutti.

Prague
9 November, 1939
(Ernst Weisz)

My dear Brother Eddie,

Last night when dear Mutti wrote you a letter, I was already asleep. I woke up at 6 in order to write to you. I must be at school around 8–9. I already speak Czech very well. Today, I was invited by our neighbor, a woman, for a noon meal, while Dad and Mom are away. I wish you the best of luck in all that you do.

Countless greetings and kisses.

Your brother, Ernst.

Prague
4 January, 1940
(Johanna Weisz)

My good beloved Eddie,

Only today did we receive your loving letter of 24 October. It took nine weeks to arrive. You can only imagine our longing as we wait for mail. I have told you repeatedly how your letters brighten our existence.

A new year has begun once again, and we are very hopeful that we will be able to see each other this year. We look forward to next New Year's Eve when you will be able to show us the sites of New York, our new home.

We were at the American Consulate today trying to gather some information about our case. The bureau information officer told us that it was not possible to determine an exact month for our departure, although he indicated that it would be sometime this year. [According to the official] we will receive a notice four months before our departure date. And so my good Eddie, no matter how difficult this is for all of us, we must be patient. We must remain healthy until our joyful reunion. My dear boy, how we long for rest: it can only be achieved through you and with you.

Now that you know the goal, you must save what you can, for we will not bring any money with us. There is so much to prepare for here, and we cannot depend upon anyone else except you. You are our hope and our salvation. The fact that you have been in [Mendel's] shop for one year is a sign that your boss is content with you. Naturally this makes us very happy and we are proud of you. When your dear father and I join you over there, we will start a new life.

Now, how did you spend your Christmas? Have you been invited by friends once again? We spent the day with our neighbors who are very good people. The relatives were with us for New Years, and I used an old family recipe to bake an "evening bread" that was enjoyed by all.

Young Ernst goes often to the skating rink. He can skate very well, and he has bought himself a hockey stick. When he said Eddie had one, I could not say anything more. He came home from the ice today very tired, and he is already sleeping. All things considered, he is doing quite well and is growing up nicely. We are amazed with our little one.

I will stop now for today. Remain healthy. Heartfelt greetings and kisses,

Your loving Mutti.

P.S. All the relatives have read your letters and they send you their greetings.

Take good care.

Once again, many, many kisses, from your Mutti who thinks of you continually.

Prague
5 January, 1940
(Heinrich Weisz)

My dear young man,

I had to wait a long time for your last letter, and unfortunately, I was not entirely satisfied with its content. Everything was treated much too briefly. You must take more time and write at least as much as we do. Nevertheless, we enjoyed these scarce lines as much as was possible.

We hope that the current year (1940) will be a joyful one for us and that our wishes will finally be granted. Now we start counting the months. Once winter has passed, we can check off another chunk of time.

Although I no longer have a head for learning, we will resume our English instruction. At my age, you can imagine that it is not so easy to zealously learn new things. As far as our health goes, we are fine and we have everything we need. Ultimately these are the truly important things.

I can also share with you that we have obtained Slovak Passes and will have to travel to Slovakia. The same thing affects all relatives.

You wrote that you went to HIAS (Hebrew Immigrant Aid Society) in order to make inquiries on our behalf. Please keep us informed about everything you do, for it will take a long time before all these formalities are taken care of. I am interested to know about your experiences there. Write to us about all of the details.

As both your dear Mutti and I have written repeatedly, we rejoice in the fact that you have done well for yourself and that you have been employed in the shop for one year. This indicates that your boss is satisfied with your performance.

I hope that this letter finds you in good health. May your next letter be longer. For today, a million heartfelt greetings from all of us.

Affectionately yours, Papa.

Prague
10 April, 1940
(Johanna Weisz)

My beloved good Eddie,

We received your dear letter with great joy. It was en route for more than three months. Every time the postman delivers a letter from you, I give him a Krone, a gesture that he is always pleased with. We were very pleased with your long letter, as you know how everything that you do interests us. We will send this letter via Budapest so that it travels faster.

Yes, my good Eddie, I do my best to take care of dear father and my loved ones just like before, even though our household is little. Sunday breakfast is still a special occasion, and it would be wonderful were we in your company being spoiled by you.

There is still no decision from the consulate. Those being allowed to leave at present received their notices in July 1938. We were not notified until October 1938. Everything takes such a long time with the consulate.

Have you received a pay raise? We are very confident that you will make your way over there, and our faith in you is great. We are tremendously proud of you.

It is now 9:00 P.M., and the little one is already asleep. He insisted that he did not want to go to bed. When I told him, however, that he needed his sleep in order to grow and impress his big brother when we are together again, he went straight to bed. He says that he will sleep in a bedroom with you and he constantly speaks of you with great pride.

Did you get the position of boxing coach? What do you earn? Have you already saved some money? My dear Eddie, we long to see you again. What do you pay for your room? When we are together, two rooms will be enough. There is no need to worry about us for now, as we have plenty to eat.

Now my dear Eddie, be well and take good care. Remain healthy for me.

Greetings and kisses.

Affectionately yours, Mutti.

Prague
10 April, 1940
(Ernst Weisz)

Dear Eddie,

I enjoyed your last letter. I think it would be boring for me to have my own room. I am pleased to have many books, and I have read many good ones. For example, Ben Hur, Till Eulenspiegel, Von Alten Frittzen, and many others that you have left for me. I have almost read them all. I also received your postcard. When you become a boxing coach, I will be your best student.

Heartfelt greetings and 5,687,587,960 kisses.

Your little brother, Ernst.

Prague
15 May, 1940
(Johanna Weisz)

My dear good Eddie,

Your two dear letters and card were received with great joy. Each letter was en route for two months, and they arrived only a few days apart. It pleases us to read that things go well with you, thanks be to God. Your dear letter of 17 March arrived today, on my birthday. You look wonderful in the picture. I have it in front of me, and I look at it first thing when I wake. The photo shows your dear good laughter and cheerful mood.

I assume that you also wrote to us in the month of February, but we did not receive any mail postmarked in February. Write to us about that time.

It is absolutely appropriate that you have changed positions, and it pleases us that you have found good people to work with. What type of business is it, and how much do you earn?

Young Ernst has truly forgotten much of his German. He writes in Czech and has little practice speaking German outside of the home. He does read German well. He looks more like you each day. Presently, he wants to have a bicycle, and then he will want something else. I tell him that you will buy him one. What he likes best of all is to put on a fresh shirt and socks every day. Dear Papa calls him "Young Lord." For Mother's Day, he gave me a flower pot. For my birthday today, Aunt Rosa and Uncle Jupp were with us. They have given me all sorts of attention. I baked a cake with nuts, just the way you like it. My dear child, I hope that I will spend my next birthday with you, as I have thought a great deal about you lately.

With whom did you spend the two Seder days [the first two nights of Passover were on 22–23 April]? Easter and the following weeks were cold for us as well.

I will close for today my dearest Eddie. Remain healthy and take good care. One year from today I will be with you in great joy.

I kiss you countless times. Affectionately, your loving Mutti.

Prague
16 August, 1940
(Johanna Weisz)

My beloved good Eddie,

We received your two dear letters of 12 and 13 July with great joy and learned of your initial successes at work. I congratulate you and wish you all the best in the future. Praise God that you have been successful in everything in all of your endeavors. God's blessing is with you my dear boy. Your good heart has enabled you to accomplish all of this. We are very pleased for you, and we are happy that your work is satisfying.

As you already know, young Ernst has been torn apart by Papa's decision to shave his head. Papa and I are being photographed by ourselves, and Ernst will be pictured on his own [for passport photos]. We will send you the pictures as quickly as possible.

The little one [Ernst] caught a cold during his trip away from home, and he returned entirely sick. He is better now, but we were really concerned.

We are making good progress in English. But I am worried that when we hear it spoken rapidly, we will not be able to follow it at all.

I can only imagine that Eli [Elias, Eddie's childhood friend who moved to New York] was saddened by your departure. But I know that you are trying to provide a position for him at your work.

Dear Eddie, I am very interested to know how much you earn and whether you have already saved some. Yes, yes, my good boy, if your beloved grandma were still living, she would have liked you very much. We still brag about your nice outings with the car [Eddie had purchased a car before moving from New York to Detroit].

Please let me know if people wear leather hosen over there; if so, I may have some made for young Ernst. I would like to have a picture of you sitting proudly in your car, but please make it a little larger than the one that you sent before. We also want to know whether you sell glasses at the firm called Brillo. [The confusion stems from the German word for glasses, *die Brille*]

Remain healthy and please drive carefully. I kiss you countless times.

Affectionately yours, Mutti.

The Successful Salesman.

[The following lines are written in English]. I like you verry much (*sic*). God bless you my good boy. Your mother. When I get a letter of you, I am happy.

Prague
31 August, 1940
(Heinrich Weisz)

My dear young man,

Today, 31 August, we received your letter dated 24 July. Comparatively speaking, this letter took fewer weeks [to arrive than previous ones], and we were very pleased to receive it. I marvel at how rapidly you have changed jobs and locations. I know how hard these transitions are for you, and I am amazed and full of admiration at how quickly you have taken upon yourself to do traveling sales. I know what it is to conduct business transactions in foreign locales for I did so myself when I was 23 years old. The first time is very boring and challenging until you have established yourself. But when you have visited a customer for the second and third time, it becomes more interesting, and the boredom, that is, being alone, does not weigh so heavily any more. Do you have to establish the contacts yourself, or are they arranged for you? Write to me about your work because all this is of interest to me. How long are you away on the road? You see, there is much to tell me. Do you receive a travel stipend? Courage my dear boy, the business will go well.

In answer to your inquiry my son, thanks be to God we are well. This is the main thing. As I read from your lines, we are failing you. We feel completely uprooted. We hope that when we are all together, things will be better for all of us.

Write to us frequently. Be well my son. All the best to you on your birthday. Be brave, courageous, and gallant so that you continue to make us very proud. Heartfelt greetings and kisses, your affectionately loving Papa.

Greetings to Aunt Sofie, Aunt Rosa, and everyone else [this, in spite of the fact that Eddie now lives in Detroit, a great distance from his relatives].

Prague
31 August, 1940
(Johanna Weisz)

My sincerely beloved good Eddie,

We received your dear letter of 24 July early this morning. Once again, we were able to rejoice. It made us sad, however, to read that you feel so lonely.

When one is used to living in a large city it is difficult to get used to a small place [the Weisz family evidently thought that Detroit was a much smaller city than it actually was]. Be patient my dear Eddie. You know that all beginnings are hard. I know that you will be successful and that your work will help to pass the time until we are with you. It goes without saying that we long tremendously to be with you, and we imagine that all will be beautiful [when we reunite]. We, too, have to wait. But it will be splendid again then.

In my thoughts I often see myself sitting next to my grown son, of whom I am so proud, in his car. You should have received our pictures for your birthday, but they will not be ready until next week. You must not feel lonely; think of this, that our thoughts and our entire love surround you. Then, my dear child, let the knowledge of all you do for us prop you up.

Now, my dear Eddie, it will soon be your birthday. I wish you good and beautiful things, all that a proud mother can wish for her beloved child. God be with you. You remain our pride and joy. I wish you all the best for the holy days and pray for good things. May God bless you and your work. Take good care and drive carefully. Be well my dear Eddie. I send hearty kisses.

Affectionately yours, Mutti.

Prague
31 August, 1940
(Ernst Weisz)

Dear Eddie,

I wish you the best for your birthday. I also wish you the best in the world for the holy days. The silver fir becomes green. May God grant you a cheerful heart dear Eddie. Many millions of greetings and kisses.

Your brother, Ernst.

One year after war erupted in Europe, Heinrich, Johanna, and Ernst Weisz's effort to reunite with Eddie remained frustrated. Their letters document the U.S. State Department's tragically effective campaign of bureaucratic delay that was instituted to stem the tide of Jewish immigration into the United States. In spite of having secured the financial affidavits necessary to enter the U.S. and processed all the required paperwork, consulate officials in Prague repeatedly stonewalled the Weisz family's efforts to leave Europe. Vague assurances of an eventual departure date at the outset of the year did not translate into a definitive approval by the end of August. Eddie and his family's repeated and increasingly desperate efforts to advance the immigration process were no match for the bureaucratic roadblocks erected by U.S. diplomats. Constant rejection and disappointment were only countered by Eddie's letters that arrived with decreasing regularity throughout the year. With little else to look forward to, Heinrich Weisz's plea for more substantive letters appears to be a modest request. So too does Johanna Weisz's supplication for more regular correspondence. After all, mail from Eddie remained her lifeline, one in which she invested all hope for the future. While no mention is ever made of food shortages or severe deprivation of any kind, conditions for Jews living in Prague during this time deteriorated with each passing day.

Housed in a two-room apartment equipped with sparse kitchen furnishings scavenged from a former building tenant, Johanna Weisz did everything possible to care for her family. She scoured the market place to secure ingredients for favorite recipes, regularly invited extended family members for meals, and she nervously observed Ernst's maturation into a young man. Johanna Weisz took great pride in her younger son's ability to adapt to the Czech speaking environment and his penchant for sport modeled on Eddie's example, although she clearly worried about the hostile environment in which they lived. While her letters do not specifically refer to antisemitic encounters, the historical record is replete with testimony that documents the abuse endured by Prague's Jewish residents. Ernst's school and sporting activities occurred within a Jewish enclave. Interaction with the non-Jewish population was limited and riddled with tensions advanced by Nazi propaganda and anti-Jewish legislation. Yet, in the midst of this threatening world, the Weisz family enjoyed sufficiently friendly relations with a few Gentile neighbors to produce an invitation to share a Christmas meal. Their existence was one of extremes: depravation and daily struggles on the one hand, countered by Eddie's successful integration into America on the other. It is little wonder that they yearned for a minute accounting of life from Eddie.

As the war progressed and time increased for letters to travel between New York and Prague, months elapsed before Eddie's family knew details about his transition to Detroit. In preparation for the move, Eddie purchased a Packard from a New York car dealer for $200. On his way home from the dealership where he had purchased the car, Eddie's pleasure with his purchase quickly dissolved when he noticed smoke coming from the car's rear. Thinking that he had been taken by a fast talking sales person, Eddie stormed back to the dealer and insisted that he had been sold a bad vehicle. It was not long, however, before the sale person figured out that Eddie had not released the hand brake and the smoke resulted from overheated brakes. After a quick lesson on operating the vehicle, Eddie left the dealership with a renewed sense of satisfaction, ready to take to the road and begin a new chapter in his life. Once relocated in Detroit, he lost little time settling into his new position. Although letters from his family indicate that Eddie struggled initially with the social isolation of road trips, it did not take long before he developed a loyal clientele and friends with whom to socialize. Not only did he make calls throughout the region to grocery and home supply stores, Eddie recognized that Detroit's rapidly expanding car wash industry was a prime market for Brillo Pads. This sales innovation brought significant income to Eddie and recognition by his superiors. Throughout 1940, Eddie remained focused on expanding his sales opportunities and getting his family out of Prague. His success in sales, however, could not mask his increasing frustration and disappointment at not being able to facilitate his family's immigration. When Eddie determined that no amount of business success would produce a reunion with his family and that his family's safety could only be guaranteed by a Nazi defeat, he changed tactics. In February 1941, Eddie enlisted in the United States Army. The time had come for him to take the fight directly to his opponent.

Chapter Seven

1941

In March 1941, Nazi Germany dominated the European continent. The German army's lightning military campaign the previous spring brought much of Western Europe under its control, through both direct occupation (Belgium, Holland, and Northern France) and collaboration (Norway and Vichy France). Although the Battle of Britain initiated in June 1940, failed to produce the total victory promised by Hermann Goering, English citizens reeled from massive aerial assaults unleashed by the German Luftwaffe. Steeled by the resolve of its recently appointed Prime Minister, Winston Churchill, Britain stood alone in the war against the Nazis. In Czechoslovakia, pressure on the Jewish community intensified as well. The Central Office for Jewish Emigration, established by Nazi decree in 1939, functioned both as a social welfare organization and the administrative authority for the Jewish community. While Hitler's military commanders finalized their plans to invade the Soviet Union, German officials in Prague ordered the Central Office for Jewish Emigration to draw up deportation lists that would be used when the Jews were evacuated from Czechoslovakia. Under these conditions, emigration prospects grew increasingly dim for Heinrich, Johanna and Ernst Weisz.

As the war progressed in Europe, U.S. military recruiters busily processed new enlistees. On March 24, 1941, Edward A. Weiss (Eddie's new, official name) stepped through the doors of a Detroit recruiting office, ready to join the United States Army. His enlistment record indicates that he entered the army as a private and signed up for a three-year tour of duty. After his paperwork was processed, Eddie was first sent to Camp Grant, Illinois, and was then shipped to Camp Roberts in California on April 2, 1941, where he endured thirteen weeks of basic training. When Eddie completed his basic training on July 1, 1941, an Army Chaplain who had befriended him helped

The new recruit at Camp Roberts California, April 1941.

Private Edward. A. Weiss.

arrange a transfer to the Reserve Army Corps so that Eddie could focus his efforts on rescuing his family from Prague. In early July, Eddie returned to Detroit to work for a wholesale food distributor and to begin, again, the process of helping his family navigate the State Department's sophisticated bureaucratic maze.

Prague
18 March, 1941
(Johanna Weisz)

My beloved good Eddie,

We received both your dear letters of 3 February and 14 February in the best of health. Thanks be to God, my good Eddie, that everything with you is also fine. We are indeed very happy that your boss is satisfied with your work. When such good news comes from you my good child, it is a holiday for us.

As you already know, the Consulate has moved to Vienna. We have sent all of our papers there, but as of today, there is still no news. They are not in a hurry. Hopefully good luck will be with us so that we can get away. It is proper that you send new papers to your former boss and do everything you can [on our behalf].

I trust that you already received the picture of us with young Ernst. I believe that you will be amazed at your brother. It has been almost three years [since you left], and a child changes much. Young Ernst will make his Bar Mitzvah in July, and I will let you know which day. We want to make the day as beautiful as possible for him. Of course it will not be possible for us to have as many guests here as we did for your Bar Mitzvah. Still, we will have a nice suit made for him but with short trousers just as you wore them. The image of you on that day is firmly implanted in my mind.

When you write to the dear Aunts, send them my greetings. Also, give our warmest regards to Mr. and Mrs. Schloss [the Schloss family had befriended Eddie when he lived in New York]. I wish that I already knew them personally so that I could share our pride for you with them. I cannot tell you often enough how unspeakably proud and happy we are of you. I dream of you often and am very pleased that this is so. I must stop in order to leave room for Young Ernst. I kiss you.

Affectionately, Mutti.

God bless you, my dear boy [written in English].

(Ernst Weisz on the same letter)

Dear Eddie.

My Bar Mitzvah is on June 14. I already know my Haftarah [the weekly prophetic reading that is chanted by the Bar Mitzvah celebrant] very well. I will think of you on my Bar Mitzvah. Dear Mama will be very busy with baking and cooking. I will therefore be as good to my parents as you are. I long for you, and I look forward to my new bicycle and to sit with you in your car. I received a very good report card. All twos. I must stop now because I have to go to school.

Remain healthy and 111,888,888,888 kisses.

Your Ernst.

(Heinrich Weisz on the same letter)

My dear young man!

Your dear writing of February 19, 1941, took about 5 weeks to arrive, and I will answer your questions in detail. There is still no answer from the American Consulate. As soon as there is something new, I will write you at once. As I have written previously, even if the Consul denies our visa, it is imperative to reserve passage on a ship. This is important above all else because little ship space to the USA is free, and the confirmation must be submitted to the Consul. We will hope for the best.

You should be very proud that your company has acknowledged your good work. It reassures me and is praiseworthy that you established yourself so well. I am confident that you will make your way. Although I was only able to translate with great difficulty the papers that you and Mr. Loeb sent, it pleased me to learn of your activities within the company.

Our hopes remain with you my dear child. We pray to God that all of us will remain healthy and the day will soon come when all of us will be together happily and contented. As I wrote previously, I received your letter two days before my birthday, which brought greater joy than the most beautiful gift. Even when you have nothing new to report, we rejoice endlessly when we have news from you.

Your dear letter dated February 19 is from Monroe. With so much free time I read books about America. I find it very interesting to learn about the Monroe Doctrine.

I am with you in thought as you make your way through large and small towns on the way.

Stay well my dear boy. I embrace and kiss you affectionately.

Papa.

Prague
14 April, 1941
(Heinrich Weisz)

Your letter came on the evening before Seder. You can imagine our joy. I have sent the affidavit and other papers from your company to the USA Consulate in Vienna. So far we have not received an answer. We hope that the Almighty will enable us to get out of here. Now, my dear son, this is the main thing. Should we be lucky enough [to receive the visas], we must postpone the confirmation of ship passage. You must confirm specifically which ship company is suitable and reserve the tickets for July. Send confirmation of this to me. This is of great significance. Without it, there is no visa.

(Johanna Weisz on the same letter)

My beloved, good Eddie,

Just as your dear father has written, your dear letter came on Seder evening. Our joy was great. I was on my way home when I met young Ernst along the way. He was radiant when he told me about the letter. You made a mistake about young Ernst's birthday on the affidavit. Instead of 26 May, [you wrote] 26 September. It is no problem.

How have you spent the Seder evening, my good Eddie? I can only think that your thoughts were with us. This is especially true on a holiday.

Pay heed when you drive. It is fine that you have begun to save money. I am unspeakably proud of you. The day must come when we will see one another. Stay healthy, this is the main thing. I say my prayers every night and morning for you. Now, my dear Eddie, all the best to you. Stay well. I kiss you many times.

Affectionately yours, Mutti.

Young Ernst is already in bed.

Prague
4 April, 1941
(Heinrich Weisz)

My dear boy,

I am very pleased that, thanks be to God, everything you undertake goes like clockwork. May you continue along your successful path as you always have. We are particularly happy that you are healthy. Thanks be to God.

Now my dear child, I return to the old fire. Even though we still have not received an answer from the Consulate, one could come any day. The matter is thus: the Consulate makes the visa dependent upon a confirmed ship reservation, which must be obtained from a ship transportation company [in the United States] that can make the appropriate reservations. All of these things must be in hand to make the application. Now see what can be done. Has your local HIAS made a decision yet [this question refers to the promise of financial support]? As you see, all of this is linked. Can you swing this as well? It is not a little thing. Now my child, carefully consider whether you can take this heavy load upon yourself.

In the meantime, we must wait. We have become used to this. The important thing is that we remain healthy. Your business success is especially gratifying. It provides consolation that you have established yourself so firmly.

Remain diligent and courageous in all that you do. There is nothing more in particular for today. Hearty greetings and kisses.

Affectionately yours, Papa.

(Ernst Weisz on the same letter)

Dear Eddie,

I want to write a few lines. I long for you, and I wish I was already with you. Tomorrow is the first of April; I will tease everyone.

Greetings and kisses.

Ernst

Prague
29 May, 1941
(Heinrich Weisz)

My dear young man!

As I have already written, we sent your affidavit and the papers from Mrs. Loeb to the Consul in Vienna. As of today, we have not received an answer. In July of this year the Czechs should begin using quotas once more, and we will then see whether we can escape. At any rate, the ship reservation is imperative. Inquire again with HIAS and the Joint [this refers to the Joint Distribution Committee, an American Jewish aid society]. Be so good my dear young man to see to it that the Aunts [Sophie and Rosa] send their affidavit as quickly as possible. They should do this by air mail so that it does not take as long to arrive here.

We are pleased that you are healthy. Thanks be to God. All is fine with us as well. Write to us at once so that we have at least this joy. There is nothing more in particular for today. Thousands of greetings and kisses.

Affectionately, your Papa.

(Johanna Weisz on the same letter.)

My deeply beloved good Eddie,

We received your dear letter with the pictures in the best of health and with great joy. It arrived on young Ernst's birthday, which doubled our joy since I had expected to receive mail from you on that day. The pictures came out all right in spite of the negative. It looks as though you are standing in snow. Next time, send us a large format so that I can look at you for hours. You look so fine and as if you have grown. Uncle Adolf will be astonished when I send him the picture.

The Czech quotas begin July 1, and we hope to be part of it. I know that you will not delay a single day in making reservations. Our longing for you is our overwhelming thought.

Young Ernst keeps dreaming about his bike. I must say that he resembles you in this respect. He torments me to buy him a bike here, but I will not do so. Please communicate this to him so that he will leave me in peace.

Remain healthy, good, and continually faithful so that you will be our joy. I am pleased that you are satisfied with your work, and I beg you, my good boy, to drive very carefully. It is already 11 at night. I kiss your dear face many, many times.

Your loving Mutti

Prague
17 June, 1941
(Johanna Weisz)

My beloved good Eddie,

Once again I wait for mail from you. The Bar Mitzvah with all of its excitement and work is over. We went to the Temple at 9:00 in the morning. While we were on our way, young Ernst remembered that he had forgotten his book and had to return home to retrieve it. He walked at my side, arm in arm, like you did [on your Bar Mitzvah] my good Eddie. When he was called to the Torah, my heart beat normally. Although this is only one step in life, he did a good job. He received nice gifts and also a travel chest. While sitting in Temple, I thought about you a great deal, my dear Eddie. I saw you sitting next to me. Instead of young Ernst on the pulpit, I saw you. I thought of you all day long and my heart was heavy. The relatives came in the afternoon, which although very nice was not as nice as yours. Nevertheless, young Ernst enjoyed himself. He also received a very inexpensive camera that will be a good one to learn on. He wants to be able to send you pictures.

Now my dear good Eddie, stay well. Many greetings and kisses.

Affectionately yours, Mutti.

(Heinrich Weisz on the same letter)

My dear good young man!

Your dear Mutti has already depicted the Bar Mitzvah for you, so once again I return to our departure. You wrote in a letter that you visited with a shipping company regarding a reservation and so forth. In inquiring here with the Jewish communal authorities, the matter has to be completed as follows. First, you are to get in touch personally with the Joint to see how inexpensively you can obtain three ship tickets. If the ship tickets are handled by the Joint, then the Joint gets in touch with the local Jewish communal authorities, and the Jewish Emigration Office in Prague undertakes all further steps needed to obtain a visa. The Consulate does not move unless one is able to present ship tickets. I understand that you can arrange everything at this time. At any rate, the Joint is correct. You do not need to pay for everything, as was the case with your departure from Berlin.

Otherwise, nothing has changed with us, and there is nothing more to write today.

I greet and kiss you affectionately. Papa

Prague
21 August, 1941
(Heinrich Weisz)

My dear good boy!

The day before yesterday I wrote you a letter, and today I must communicate something important. It has to do with our departure. We have been told by the local authorities that new decisions have recently been made. All affidavits issued before 1 July 1941 are invalid. This is what now needs to be done. You must submit a petition to Washington that includes the dates we registered in

Prague for the Czech quotas issued from 18 October 1938 to the present, along with figures about your current gross income. Mr. Rom and Mr. Loeb must also promise their financial support. The copy of the ship tickets must also be enclosed. It is best to turn this over to the Detroit HIAS so that things move faster. The earlier that you do this my child, the better it will be.

Today I received news from dear Aunt Zilly in Vienna that Rudy can send food packages once a month that can include one kilo of coffee and other things. This could be of use to us. The procedure is as follows. There are several firms or banks that can fill these orders. You pay ten dollars to a firm in Vienna, which then sends a package to us through a firm in Germany. I believe the North German Lloyd Bremen handles these matters. You should inquire with a large bank [in the United States] to learn more details. You know that I like to drink coffee. I still have more to write, but we will wait for your prompt reply. Stay healthy.

Greetings and kisses. Affectionately yours, Papa.

(Johanna Weisz on the same letter)

My dear good Eddie,

Dear Papa has already written everything, so not much remains for me. I know we expect much of you, but ultimately your efforts will be rewarded, and it will please us greatly to receive all the necessary papers. I would be very happy if you could send us such a package. May God grant you continued good luck.

Take good care of yourself. I kiss you many many times in great love.

Your mother [written in English].

Prague
24 October, 1941
(Johanna Weisz)

My dear good Eddie!

We received mail again after a long while and our joy was great. Two letters came at once. One that Aunt Rosa helped to write and the other which you sent from Detroit. Enclosed are a few pictures taken on our street in front of our house. These will certainly please you and let you see the path we walk.

My dear Eddie, do me a favor and write punctually every week. I am killing myself with worries. You remember of course that when you were at home, I could not go to sleep before I heard your steps. Here I get no rest when I do not receive mail from you.

We are healthy and our main wish is to stay well. In only a year and a half you will become a citizen and then they will finally have to let us in. Do you have any news about the application from Washington? These gentlemen are not in as much of a hurry as we are. I wonder whether the son of Uncle Armin, who is a civil servant, could do something. One must consider all possibilities.

We often get together with Uncle Bernhard who lives in the same neighborhood as us. During the summer Uncle B. worked construction doing very heavy labor, but he is healthy. Erich [Uncle Bernhard's son] works in a locksmith shop. He earns ten Krone per week, and he rips up more than that in shoe leather. He does not want to go to school. Your brother also has no desire to go to school, but he must. He speaks and reads Czech fluently. He says he will speak Czech when he does not want you to understand him.

My good Eddie, I look forward to sharing a home with you. Do you see my dearest child how this hope gives us courage and strength. I would cook all of your favorite food and Fridays, when you return from your sales trips, would be especially beautiful. Be careful when you drive. We are pleased with your professional success, and we are unspeakably proud and happy with you. I could write much more, but young Ernst also wants to write. Stay well. I kiss you innumerable times.

Affectionately yours, Mutti.

(Ernst Weisz on the same letter)

Dear Eddie,

Here are four little pictures that I took. Hopefully you will like them. Forgive me that I write so little and so badly. I am indeed tired. It is already 11:00 P.M. So good night and 1,000,000,000 kisses.

Your Ernst.

Prague,
11 November, 1941
(Heinrich Weisz)

My beloved good Eddie,

We have received your dear letter of 10 October with great joy. In the meantime, you have received our various letters and also the telegram. Now, my good Eddie, I will only say to you not to be worried when things do not go as planned. It is important to sleep well, and do not neglect the business. In the same way, we will abide our time. I know that we have demanded a great deal of you. Once again my dearest Eddie, do not worry on our account. We are healthy and have what we need.

It is cold over here and it has already snowed. This is how it goes. I am pleased that you have been there almost three and a half years. After another year and a half, you will be a citizen and the way will be open for us to join you, my beloved son. During this period of time, you will have saved even more money. Dear Eddie, if possible please write to us every week. I am interested in all that you do, and I read your letters often. I already have an entire pile.

Do you have any news from Washington? I know my dear Eddie that you wait for this without hope, just as we have waited for news from the Consulate. Unfortunately, they are not in a hurry and there is little that we can do. We count the months until you will have the rights of citizenship. This is our hope.

It will soon be Christmas again. Enjoy your vacation, my dear Eddie. I am very pleased with your business success, and I wish you all the best. There is nothing more for today. I greet and kiss you, and I am always with you in your thoughts. Take good care along your way.

Affectionately yours, Mutti.

(from Ernst)

Dear Eddie,

It is 8:00 A.M. and I must be at school at 9. I will write you a long letter next time. 15678910 greetings and kisses.

Ernst.

(from Heinrich Weisz)

My dear, dear young man!

I do not want to write every detail so that I can I write as punctually and quickly as I can. It pleases me that you have made such fast progress with the Brillo Company. Hopefully, you will advance to the top. I am very pleased with your industriousness and good success. Reflect carefully on all that you have achieved before you consider changing places.

We would like to be near you. Perhaps it is not impossible that you could visit us. We will see how this works out. In the event that it does not, do not be troubled my son or neglect your obligations. Be well and full of courage.

Please write each week so that we can enjoy receiving letters from you in a punctual and regular manner.

There is nothing more in particular to write today. I greet and kiss you warmly.

Farewell and remain healthy.

Affectionately yours, Papa.

Although Eddie did not know it when he received this letter, his father's farewell was final. It was the last communication from his family. Throughout 1941, their correspondence focused increasingly on efforts to escape the Nazi stranglehold. Eddie's parents, particularly his father, detailed the steps

Detroit, 1941.

that Eddie needed to take to facilitate their emigration. At each turn, the cal-culated bureaucratic delay choreographed by the U.S. State Department frus-trated every effort. Time and again, Heinrich and Johanna Weisz lamented the slow pace of consular officials who "were in no hurry" to expedite their ap-plication. When it appeared that everything had been properly arranged—tickets reserved, affidavits secured, passport pictures taken, and applications filed—new instructions were issued that required the Weisz family to begin the process anew. Heinrich Weisz's failure to orchestrate his family's depar-ture weighed heavily on the family patriarch, and a sense of resignation is pal-pable in his last letter when he mentions the possibility of Eddie visiting them in Prague. Both Heinrich and Johanna Weisz came to recognize that escape from Europe was dependent upon Eddie becoming a U.S. citizen. Unfortu-nately, this would occur too late to save the Weisz family.

With life's circumstances reduced significantly, Heinrich and Johanna Weisz took solace in their children's success and maturation. Eddie's business accomplishments and rapid adjustment to life in America were particular points of pride. Hungry for detailed accounts of his work and travels, Hein-rich Weisz lived vicariously through his son's experiences. Eddie's travels throughout his Midwestern sales territory served as a geography lesson for his father, and both parents were acutely aware that Eddie's success was critical to the family's future plans. Johanna Weisz eagerly anticipated caring for her son in the same manner that she had supported her husband's sales career: cooking his favorite foods and welcoming him home after a week's travel with special Friday meals to celebrate the Sabbath. Plans for the future were accompanied with reflections on Ernst's personal development, each step of which was compared to Eddie's childhood. The June Bar Mitzvah precipi-tated emotional reflections on Eddie, and Johanna Weisz compared every as-pect of the day to his celebration in 1933. She ordered Ernst a new suit of clothes similar in style to Eddie's; she prepared special food and hosted rela-tives at their home in the afternoon following the morning service as she had done for Eddie; and when Ernst was called to the Torah, Johanna Weisz visu-alized Eddie on the pulpit and not Ernst. The longing for Eddie enveloped Jo-hanna Weisz throughout the day, and it is clear that Ernst's Bar Mitzvah pro-vided a painful reminder of how life had radically changed in a few short years. She must have sensed that the parental hope for a healthy and prosper-ous future that is central to a Bar Mitzvah celebration would not be afforded to her younger son. Her self described "heavy heart" signals the increased un-certainty that shrouded the Weisz family's daily existence.

The most intriguing aspect about the final year's correspondence is the ab-sence of any mention of Eddie having enlisted in the U.S. army. Given the detailed commentary about Eddie's life contained in his parents' letters, it is

inconceivable that they would not have written about Eddie's decision to become a soldier had they known about the situation. After all, it fundamen-
tally altered plans for Eddie to financially support his parents and brother.
When asked, Eddie explained that he intentionally omitted referring to his
army enlistment, and he remains uncertain whether he even wrote to his family during basic training. Eddie feared that if Nazi censors read his letters and
learned that he had joined the U.S. army, his family would be endangered.
For this reason, Heinrich, Johanna, and Ernst Weisz never learned about Eddie's decision to join the army, a transformative event that dictated his life's
activities until the end of 1946. Once in the army, efforts to rescue his family took him to the shores of Europe and, eventually, to Prague itself, where
he searched for clues about his father, mother, and brother. The book's final
chapter details this journey.

Chapter Eight

The Search for Eddie's Family

Shortly after Eddie received the letter dated 11 November, 1941, the complexion of World War II changed significantly. The German invasion of the Soviet Union stalled in late November, and the Red Army launched a major counter offensive on December 6th. The Japanese aerial assault on Pearl Harbor the following day had immediate consequences. Not only did it precipitate the United States' declaration of war against Japan and Germany, it also forced Reinhard Heydrich, Heinrich Himmler's right-hand man, to postpone the planned meeting to coordinate the "final solution of the Jewish Question in Europe" that was scheduled for December 9th. Six weeks later, on January 20, 1942, fifteen high-ranking members of the Nazi party and German government leaders attended a two-hour meeting in a lakeside villa on the outskirts of Berlin known as Wannsee. They had been summoned to Berlin to discuss the "Final Solution," the code name for the genocide of European Jewry. While this meeting did not initiate the Final Solution, it marked the moment when Heydrich presented the plan to transport Jews from German-occupied Europe to killing centers in Poland. When the first transports arrived at the Belzec death camp in March 1942, seventy-five percent of the 6 million Jews killed during the Holocaust were still alive. Eleven months later, more than 4.5 million European Jewish men, women, and children had been murdered by the Nazis and their accomplices. The fate of Heinrich, Johanna, and Ernst Weisz was linked to this unprecedented killing campaign.

America's entrance into the war required a massive mobilization of men, a development that led to Eddie's reactivation in August 1942. Upon being recalled, Eddie was sent to Fort Benning, Georgia, to join the 10th Armor Division and subsequently transferred to the military intelligence training center at Camp Ritchie, Maryland. The federal government had activated the camp in June 1942, as a War Department Military Intelligence Training Center, and it became a training ground for thousands of German Jews like Eddie whose language skills proved invaluable in prosecuting the war against Nazi Germany. At Camp Ritchie, Eddie was trained to interrogate military prisoners in preparation for the invasion planned for 1944. While at Ritchie, Eddie also became a U.S. citizen, an event vividly etched in his memory. He recalls that when filling out the paperwork he was asked about his middle name. Since it was not customary among German Jews to use middle names, he did not know how to respond. The woman helping him process the application informed Eddie that everybody in America has a middle name and one was required to process his citizenship paperwork. Eddie asked the woman who was processing his application about her husband's middle name, to which she replied, "Alfred." When his citizenship papers were completed, they read Edward Alfred Weiss. Following his stay at Ritchie, Eddie received additional interrogation training with the Chicago police force. He was billeted at a lake front hotel, a significant step up in comfort compared to the barracks at Camp Ritchie, and he spent two months in Chicago before being shipped overseas to England in spring 1944.

While in London, Eddie was occupied during the day translating documents for the American Embassy. Even though the city was bombed frequently and life's regular routines had been disrupted, he spent his free time becoming acquainted with London. Foremost on his mind, however, was his family. He had not heard from them for two and a half years, and he anxiously awaited the opportunity to search for them himself. On June 6, 1944, Eddie's military unit, the 29th infantry, landed on Omaha Beach. It was D-Day plus two, and in spite of the fact that American forces had established a beachhead following the initial assault, German troops still peppered the beach with machine gun fire when Eddie disembarked. The boat carrying Eddie's infantry unit was not able to land close enough to the beach for the men to easily wade ashore. Like thousands of American soldiers involved in the D-Day assault, Eddie swam ashore laden with heavy equipment. A few men drowned and others, only a couple of feet away from Eddie, were gunned down. Once on the beach, Eddie scampered for cover and eventually joined forces with the 29th infantry.

Since some time passed before the American army made significant headway into France and captured German soldiers, Eddie's work as a field interrogator did not begin immediately. Throughout the months that he interviewed German prisoners of war, Eddie remained acutely aware of the link between 'Germans' and his family's fate. He insists that he never abused a prisoner of war, and he adhered to the principle that "two wrongs did not make a right." In fact, Eddie recognized that not all Germans were enemies. As the war pro-

Interrogating German War Criminals.

gressed Eddie's unit arrived in Wiesbaden, a spa town located southwest of Frankfurt, where he was befriended by a detainee that he had interrogated. Eddie is not certain why the man was arrested. He "was not much of a Nazi," but was in charge of the local veteran of foreign wars organization. One evening while in Wiesbaden, Eddie was invited to the man's family home for dinner and spent the night discussing the war, the fate of German Jews, and Eddie's family. It had been three years since he last heard from his parents.

When the war in Europe ended in May 1945, Eddie's unit was in Berlin. With the complete collapse of Germany's government and the country's subsequent military occupation, his interrogation duties were expanded to support the Allied powers' denazification efforts. Coming face to face with Nazi officials presented a new challenge for Eddie, one that tested his professionalism. On one occasion, while interviewing a man who was reputed to have been in charge of Jewish affairs for the city of Prague, Eddie's emotions got the best of him. During the interrogation, he "picked the guy up and smacked him." Sixty years later Eddie quietly admitted that this was the only time that he "completely lost his cool." The man was a member of the Gestapo, the Nazi police force notorious for its treatment of Jews and other "enemies of the Reich." Questioning a man possibly responsible for his family's disappearance simply overwhelmed him.

Toward the end of summer, Eddie received the opportunity that he had waited years for—permission to search for his family. His commanding officer provided him a jeep, a rifle, food rations, blankets, clothing, and time away from the unit. Before leaving, the colonel told Eddie, "I hope you find them. If you don't find them, give it [the rations] to the people that need it. Don't sell it on the black market." From Berlin, Eddie traveled to Prague and immediately went to the last address that he had for his family. Here he saw the furnished one room flat where they lived and met the man who rented them the room. The former landlord told Eddie that years earlier his family had been deported to Theresienstadt, the Nazi ghetto located outside the city. He described their journey to an assembly point within the city and how they were loaded into railroad cars used to transport animals. It turns out that sometime in early 1942, Eddie received a telegram reputedly sent by his parents from Theresienstadt saying that "everything is OK." He suspected at the time, and confirmed later, that the telegram was a fraud. It had been sent by Nazi ghetto officials to placate family members worried about their relatives.

The trip to Prague was bittersweet for Eddie. Standing in the apartment talking to the landlord, he could imagine being with his family. His parents' letters had detailed their daily routines, including the foods they ate, and Eddie pictured himself sharing a Sabbath meal with his father, mother, and brother. The cherished memory of fresh-baked challah and meal-time laughter clashed violently

Enjoying a smoke.

with the image of his loved ones being forced to board a cattle car. By this time, Eddie had heard stories of liberated concentration camps overflowing with emaciated and sick survivors, and he knew that untold numbers of Jews had disappeared from their homes throughout Europe. He had also read articles in the army newspaper, *Stars and Stripes*, which documented General Eisenhower's visit to the camps. And, he had seen how Jews housed in the recently created DP (Displaced Persons) camps exacted revenge upon Germans when given the opportunity. Yet, he remained hopeful that he would find his family and fulfill their dream of a life together in the United States. It had been seven years since he boarded a train from Berlin to Hamburg and said good-bye to his family. Much had happened to Eddie during this period and standing in his family's former Prague apartment, he wrestled with his emotions. His search had gone cold.

Herbert Schloss and Eddie in an East Coast pipe shop.

The Medico Company's California salesman.

Following the visit to Prague, Eddie returned to Berlin and was discharged from the army the following year, on December 12, 1946. Upon separating from the army and leaving Camp Atterbury, Indiana, he visited friends in New York and began the process of adjusting to civilian life. Eddie wasted no time getting in touch with Herbert and Arlene Schloss, the couple who had befriended him shortly after he arrived in the United States and were instrumental in helping him secure the job with Brillo in Detroit. Mr. and Mrs. Schloss warmly welcomed Eddie into their home and were anxious to learn of his wartime experiences, especially efforts to locate his family. Picking up where they left off years before, Herbert and Arlene Schloss provided emotional support and a surrogate family environment for Eddie, and helped him secure a new job. Eddie was hired by Medico Pipes, Herbert Schloss's company. Mr. Schloss had introduced Eddie to pipe smoking when the two first met in 1939, and he secured a sales position for him in California in spite of his regional manager's concerns about Eddie's strong German accent. Eddie was trained in New York before traveling to California in 1947 to begin a new life. In so doing, he returned to the environment that he had grown fond of during his basic training days at Camp Roberts.

Once settled in California, Eddie renewed the search for his family. At this point in time, however, the methods and expected outcome were different than they were during the war. Beginning in 1948, Eddie wrote letters to international agencies seeking information about his family following their deportation to Theresienstadt. A myriad of organizations, including the Red Cross, provided aid for millions of refugees left homeless by the war's destruction and the forced relocation programs of recently reconstituted nations formed under a Cold War umbrella. In addition, they assisted thousands of Holocaust survivors who were temporarily housed in Displaced Persons (DP) Camps. With the establishment of the Israeli state in May 1948, many Jews living in DP camps made their way to Israel, while others secured visas to settle in the United States, Canada, and South America. Others preferred to remain in Europe and rebuild their lives on more familiar soil. In addition to the Red Cross, Eddie communicated with the Jewish Agency for Palestine, the U.S. Department of State, the German Red Cross that was founded following the creation of the Federal Republic of Germany in 1949, the Hebrew Sheltering and Immigrant Aid Society, and many others. For four years he received polite, bureaucratic replies that offered no news of his family and typically referred him to another agency. Finally, in May 1953, he received the following letter from the International Committee of the Red Cross:

Dear Sir,

Further to your inquiry dated 25 November, 1952, we regret to inform you that we have received the following reply from the International Tracing Agency in Arlosen:

WEISZ Heinrich, born 24 February, 1880,
WEISZ Johanna, nee Lobl, born 15 May, 1892, and
WEISZ Ernst, born 26 May, 1928

were transferred with Transport: AS-736, 737, 738 on 30 April, 1942, to Zamose. Transport "AS," dated 30 April, 1942, is considered by the Czechoslovak Ministry of Social Welfare, Prague, as a death-transport from which less than 10% are known to have returned after the war."

With all our sympathy for these sad news,
Faithfully yours,
(signature is illegible)

In spite of the fact that Eddie 'knew' that his family was no longer alive, he had held out hope for a miracle. The information communicated in this letter devastated him. Not only did it confirm that his father, mother, and brother were dead, but it also shattered the dream of a reunion with his family. Eddie's search for his family was over. Heinrich, Johanna, and Ernst Weisz had been murdered by the Nazis. They were three of the six million Jews killed during the Holocaust.

Epilogue

By the time that Eddie received the letter from the International Committee of the Red Cross that detailed his family's deportation on a "death transport," he had already begun the process of rebuilding a family. In August 1950, he married Joanne Pickus. The following year, Joanne gave birth to their first child, Henry "Hank" Weiss, named in memory of Eddie's father, Heinrich. Two years later, Andrew Ernst Weiss was born, named in memory of Eddie's brother, and in 1960, Nancy Johanna Weiss entered the world, a daughter named in memory of Eddie's mother. Raised in the Weiss household, Eddie's children knew that their father's family had been killed in the Holocaust, but they were not familiar with the details of their demise or Eddie's personal history. Like many Holocaust survivors, Eddie did not openly discuss the past with his children, and he preferred, instead, to focus on the present. His daily ritual of saying good night to his father, mother, and brother while looking at their photo did not detract from his complete devotion to his wife and children. Since his marriage to Joanne in 1950, Eddie has been passionately committed to his family, even during difficult situations. When Eddie and Joanne became estranged from their eldest son and months passed without hearing from him, Eddie would not consider severing the relationship. For the past ten years, Eddie has cared for his ailing wife and refused to abandon hope for her recovery. For Eddie, each day with family is precious. Experience has taught him to cherish the lives of loved ones. This is Eddie's testimonial, a living memorial to the lives extinguished by the Nazis.

Joanne Pickus.

Index

www.ingramcontent.com/pod-product-compliance
Lightning Source LLC
Chambersburg PA
CBHW021821270326
41932CB00007B/290